Better together

A

take up & READ

PUBLICATION

Published by The Word Among Us Press
7115 Guilford Drive, Suite 100
Frederick, Maryland 21704
www.wau.org

23 22 21 20 19   1 2 3 4 5

ISBN: 978-1-59325-362-2

Nihil Obstat: Msgr. Michael Morgan, J.D., J.C.L.
                Censor Librorum
                April 9, 2019

Imprimatur: +Most Rev. Felipe J. Estevez, S.T.D.
                Diocese of St. Augustine
                April 9, 2019

Editorial Director: Elizabeth Foss
Copy Editor: Rosie Hill
Editorial Assistant: Emily DeArdo
Cover Art Photography, Illustration & Design: Kristin Foss
Research & Development: Elizabeth Foss, Colleen Connell

Made and printed in the United States of America

Library of Congress Control Number: 2019938846

take up & READ

C O M M U N I T Y

VISIT US
takeupandread.org

BE SOCIAL
Facebook @takeupandread
Instagram @takeupandread
Twitter @totakeupandread

SEND A NOTE
totakeupandread@gmail.com

CONNECT
#TakeUpAndRead
#BetterTogetherStudy

Start.

I am about to do a new thing;
   now it springs forth, do you not perceive it?
I will make a way in the wilderness
   and rivers in the desert.

ISAIAH 43:19

START DATE	PLACE

I'M FEELING

- ○ happy
- ○ excited
- ○ joyful

- ○ anxious
- ○ upset
- ○ tired

- ○ annoyed
- ○ angry
- ○ sad

- ○ grateful
- ○ confused
- ○ calm

- ○ _____
- ○ _____
- ○ _____

Outside my window:

Pondering:

Giving thanks for:

Clothed in:

Listening to:

In my prayers:

My hope for *Better Together*:

Introduction

A curious thing happened when we published a Bible study on friendship. We heard from countless women who were afraid to open the journal because they didn't think they had friends to study it with them. One woman after another confided that they were sure that a Bible study on friendship would make them feel even more alone, longing for something other women had but they did not.

What those women missed is that Jesus' kingdom is not of this world, and so everything seems upside-down. It's the women who don't think they have friends who need to see what God says about friends, who need to understand that he is their first friend and that he has a plan for all the rest of the friends. And so it is with community.

We think we don't have community. Or we think that we don't need community. Or we think that the community we know and love is all he wants for us. But God actually has a lot to say about community, and it will take us a lifetime to live out his vision for us.

People have asked us if this is a book about community or a book about hospitality. We emphatically and joyfully answer, "Yes!"

It is both. It is a book that shows God's plan for his people together and also gives you tangible tools for gracious hospitality that opens the door to community. It is a journal that asks you to thoughtfully consider your own world and to see how he might be calling you to be his hands and feet in it. This book is about extending hospitality in order to foster and nurture community. It is an invitation to live a life of abundance that is **better** for being **together**.

This book
is about
extending
hospitality in
order to foster
and nurture
community.
It is an
invitation to
live a life of
abundance
that is **better**
for being
together.

From the designer

Better Together is a quilted picnic blanket of a book, brought to you by some of the most welcoming women I know. Each contributor offered something new to this journal, and after seeing all of the pieces laid out, I found small bits of "yarn and fabric" from my own experience of community to tie all of it together.

We made a variety of new tools to help you look at your community differently. We created charts to fill in so that you can visualize what your community and support system look like. You'll find recipes and tutorials that can make any ordinary gathering special and unique. There are tips on how to make welcome in your home without spending money. Last, we added pencil illustrations and handwritten pieces throughout this book to make it feel personal and welcoming.

My hope for *Better Together* is to help bring community your way, in a joyous and bright light.

Kristin Foss, Designer

intentional design

In this Scripture study, we explore hospitality and community within the Bible. We added extra tools to help you define what community looks like in your life and how to identify your support system. We designed a journaling layout to help you examine community with a special focus on gratitude. Enjoy the extra recipes, tutorials, and tools to help you create community through hospitality.

DAILY READINGS

Join us in daily readings, which shed light on how God wants us to rejoice in hospitality and community.

SELAH

Take a day for pause in your Scripture study on Selah days and check in with yourself and your community.

WEEKLY SCRIPTURE VERSE

Each week has a focus Scripture to hide in your heart throughout the week.

Who is your neighbor?

Scripture Memory

When we memorize Scripture, we imitate Jesus, who hid God's word in his heart and who proclaimed it even in his most sorrowful agony. As he hung in the final moments of his life, Scripture was the last thing on his breath, and Jesus, "crying with a loud voice, said, 'Father, into your hands I.commend my spirit.' Having said .this, he breathed his last" (Luke 23:46). We can almost certainly know that Jesus learned those words from Psalm 31 from his mother as a prayer when he was a little boy. She poured into him a treasury of Scripture and he knew just where to find it all his life.

To hold the word of God so close and so dear that it is what sustains us in the very last moments of our lives! To hide the Lord in our hearts in such a real and present way that he spills out into our speech when we are neediest and when we are most joyful! These are the true goals of the Take Up & Read studies.

Each week, we offer a memory verse for you to hide in your heart, and perhaps in the hearts of children too. This week, we focus on the apostles in the early Church and their devotion to the Lord and to one another.

All who believed were together and had all things in common; they would sell their possessions and goods and distribute the proceeds to all, as any had need. Day by day, as they spent much time together in the temple, they broke bread at home and ate their food with glad and generous hearts, praising God and having the goodwill of all the people. And day by day the Lord added to their number those who were being saved.

ACTS 2: 44-47

Who is your neighbor?

SCRIPTURE MEMORY

> Day by day, as they spent much time together in the temple, they
> broke bread at home and ate their food with glad and generous hearts,
> praising God and having the goodwill of all the people.
>
> ACTS 2:46-47

I will practice Scripture memory by
- ○ Praying
- ○ Writing
- ○ Speaking
- ○ Reading
- ○ Other: _____

PUMPKIN MUFFINS

Ingredients

- ◯ 2 cups all-purpose flour or two cups gluten-free all-purpose flour (we prefer Namaste)
- ◯ 1 teaspoon nutmeg
- ◯ 1 teaspoon ground cinnamon
- ◯ 1 teaspoon ground cloves
- ◯ ½ teaspoon baking powder
- ◯ 1 teaspoon baking soda
- ◯ ½ teaspoon salt
- ◯ 1 ½ sticks butter (¾ cup), softened
- ◯ 1 ¾ cups sugar
- ◯ 3 large eggs
- ◯ 1 15-ounce can 100% pure pumpkin (not pumpkin pie filling)

These are as nice tucked into a picnic basket in July as they are with hot spiced cider in the fall. Don't limit pumpkin to November!

Directions

Set the oven rack in the middle position and preheat the oven to 325°F. Grease and flour 24 muffin cups or use muffin papers. Alternatively, generously grease two 8X4-inch loaf pans with butter and dust with flour.

In a medium bowl, combine flour, nutmeg, cinnamon, cloves, baking powder, baking soda, and salt. Set aside.

In a large bowl suitable for an electric stand mixer or handheld electric beaters, beat the butter and sugar until blended well. Add the eggs, one at a time, beating after each addition. Continue to beat the sugar, butter, and egg mixture until the mixture is light and fluffy. Beat in the pumpkin. If the mixture looks a little curdled, it's fine.

Add the flour mixture, a little at a time, and mix on low speed until all is combined. Do not overmix.

Divide the batter evenly among the muffin cups or loaf pans.

Bake muffins for about 35-40 minutes or loaves for 65 minutes, until a toothpick inserted into the middle comes out clean.

Let the muffins or loaves cool in the pans for about 10 minutes. Turn out onto a wire rack to cool completely.

ACTS 2:44-47

All who believed were together and had all things in common; they would sell their possessions and goods and distribute the proceeds to all, as any had need. Day by day, as they spent much time together in the temple, they broke bread at home and ate their food with glad and generous hearts, praising God and having the goodwill of all the people. And day by day the Lord added to their number those who were being saved.

For further reading:
Hebrews 3:12-13
Hebrews 10:24-25
John 13:35

With the Book of Acts, St. Luke continues his narration of the story of Jesus by spilling it over into the life of the early Church. In an earlier verse before today's reading, St. Luke relates how St. Peter has told the crowds to reform their lives, to repent and be baptized:

And so, "those who welcomed his message were baptized, and that day about three thousand persons were added" (Acts 2:41).

Under the power of the Holy Spirit, the newly baptized convened to do life together. Their baptism was a momentous public event, followed directly by the daily disciplines we read about in today's verses.

Take a few moments at the beginning of this study to consider the daily disciplines in your life.

When you were baptized, the Holy Spirit breathed new life into you. How do your daily disciplines nurture that life in your own soul and in your community?

What is life-giving? Where do you see room to grow?

Day Two

I see it in her face, this little girl on the cusp of being a teenager, and I ache for her. Briefly, I think of all the ways I have tried to frame her life to avoid moments like these. And then I think about how futile—and even how wrong—it was to even try. She has been hurt by her little tribe of friends, and the tension that plays across her face and settles into the deep furrows and leaks out her eyes is the tension every woman has known. Which is better, to be lonely or to be wounded?

The answer, of course, is to be wounded. We were created to be wounded. We're not in this alone, and we can't do it alone; that is, we cannot become more like Christ without being surrounded and in community with the imperfect people who try our souls and challenge us to grow in charity.

We need people who help us believe. We need to live deeply invested in those relationships. And we need to bear witness to the fullness of the body of Christ to a broken world. We need awe to infuse our souls and capture our hearts for Christ. Then, we need to allow ourselves to be moved by our awesome God together.

The early apostles were a rich, vibrant community that lived closely with one another. We know that they worshipped together and they were nourished by the Eucharist together and they met one another's material needs. God granted grace to each member of that early community and each member extended it to one another.

This is the gospel. This is what God intends for us.

God wants for us to live in community, devoted to one another and devoted to the Lord. In this brief passage, St. Luke has penned the Holy Spirit's description of a community of faith for our sake. Everything we need to know is here. In these four verses, we know what brought and held believers together in the early years of the Church, what inspired them to live lives entirely devoted to following the risen Christ, and what the legacy of their sacrificial faith means for us now.

I've committed these verses to memory, and sometimes I idealize them in my mind. The early Christians all seemed to live heartily unto the Lord, wholly committed to Christ and to one another. There were no twelve-year-old mean girls and no fully grown women tearing each other apart.

Except there were.

Christ lived among sinners, and when he died, those sinners were sinners still. We cannot learn to love the way Christ did unless we keep company with sinners. God calls the sinners together to live in close community, bumping up against one another, making disciples of one another before we look beyond our closeness and out into the nations.

At our tables and in our homes, we are offered the opportunity to welcome and to embrace the imperfect people whom God has intended to do life with us.

Sliding down to make room in the pew, we acknowledge together before the altar that we are a community that will disappoint each other, daily surrendered to a Lord who showers us with unearned mercy and shows us how to extend that mercy to one another. We cannot grow in holiness wholly alone. We need each other.

When I play out my idealized community of daydreams, there is a sisterhood of kindred spirits united in purpose and grace. On good days, that dream has roots in reality. But on difficult days—and there will be difficult days—there is pain and there are tears and the daydream fades into disappointment. This too is fruitful community. It is here, together, that we learn to reconcile and it is towards each other that we extend forgiveness.

Life offers us limitless opportunities to love imperfect people. Christ's call to community isn't just for the few who have the near-perfect small group within a near-perfect parish. It's for all of us. He asks us to know that to be wounded because we reached out in love is to be with him intimately. His grace will be abundant as he assures us that it is always better to love. Always. Don't be afraid to be vulnerable enough to do life with others.

He calls us to be better together.

Elizabeth Foss

LUKE 10:25-37

Just then a lawyer stood up to test Jesus. "Teacher," he said, "what must I do to inherit eternal life?" He said to him, "What is written in the law? What do you read there?" He answered, "You shall love the Lord your God with all your heart, and with all your soul, and with all your strength, and with all your mind; and your neighbor as yourself." And he said to him, "You have given the right answer; do this, and you will live." But wanting to justify himself, he asked Jesus, "And who is my neighbor?" Jesus replied, "A man was going down from Jerusalem to Jericho, and fell into the hands of robbers, who stripped him, beat him, and went away, leaving him half dead. Now by chance a priest was going down that road; and when he saw him, he passed by on the other side. So likewise a Levite, when he came to the place and saw him, passed by on the other side. But a Samaritan while traveling came near him; and when he saw him, he was moved with pity. He went to him and bandaged his wounds, having poured oil and wine on them. Then he put him on his own animal, brought him to an inn, and took care of him. The next day he took out two denarii, gave them to the innkeeper, and said, 'Take care of him; and when I come back, I will repay you whatever more you spend.' Which of these three, do you think, was a neighbor to the man who fell into the hands of the robbers?" He said, "The one who showed him mercy." Jesus said to him, "Go and do likewise."

EPHESIANS 2:10

For we are what he has made us, created in Christ Jesus for good works, which God prepared beforehand to be our way of life.

For further reading:
Leviticus 19:33-34
Luke 14:12-14

REACH OUT   RESOLVE   REJOICE

How can you reach someone inside of your circles today?

How will you live out what God has shared with your heart in today's reading?

Count three blessings:

How can you reach outside of your circles today?

Ways I fostered community today: Prayer Intentions

- ○ prayed for a friend
- ○ put down my phone in the presence of people
- ○ made plans to host a gathering
- ○ replied "yes" to an invitation
- ○ hugged someone important to me
- ○ shared a meal with someone special
- ○ wrote a letter by hand
- ○ set a table for more than myself
- ○ introduced myself to someone new
- ○ made time for these people:

- ○ other:

Asking God's help for myself:

Day Three

When we begin to ponder intentional hospitality and the purpose of living as Christ in community with one another, it is perhaps a good exercise to understand that Christ exhorts us to love our neighbor as ourselves and then to ask who, exactly, is our neighbor. To do that, though, is to risk missing the point of the parable.

Christ isn't telling the lawyer that the man going to Jericho who was beaten and left for dead is his neighbor. Instead, he's turning the question on its end. He's asking the lawyer if he can be a neighbor. Don't spend too much time trying to determine who is your neighbor; instead, spend that time asking our Lord, *What kind of person am I? Am I a neighbor to each and every person you put in my life? Can I act with mercy, no matter what, no matter when?*

Long before modern cries for justice and colored ribbons for causes and crowd funding, C. S. Lewis observed that each and every person we meet will one day glory in heaven or suffer in hell.

It is a serious thing to live in a society of possible gods and goddesses, to remember that the dullest most uninteresting person you can talk to may one day be a creature which, if you saw it now, you would be strongly tempted to worship, or else a horror and a corruption such as you now meet, if at all, only in a nightmare. All day long we are, in some degree helping each other to one or the other of these destinations. It is in the light of these overwhelming possibilities, it is with the awe and the circumspection proper to them, that we should conduct all of our dealings with one another, all friendships, all loves, all play, all politics. There are no ordinary people. You have never talked to a mere mortal. Nations, cultures, arts, civilizations—these are mortal, and their life is to ours as the life of a gnat. But it is immortals whom we joke with, work with, marry, snub, and exploit—immortal horrors or everlasting splendors. This does not mean that we are to be perpetually solemn. We must play. But our merriment must be of that kind (and it is, in fact, the merriest kind) which exists between people who have, from the outset, taken each other seriously—no flippancy, no superiority, no presumption. (C. S. Lewis, *The Weight of Glory*)

Our neighbor is the next person we meet. Will a child come downstairs shortly, with bedhead and morning breath, needing breakfast right away? You will look up, close this book, greet him with merriment and be glad to have such an easy neighbor to encounter first thing. And then, as you move in concentric circles from your home, you will encounter every sort of neighbor, looking at them with eyes opened by the gospel. You will do your part—whatever it is—to bring to them the light of Christ so that they, with you, can be "everlasting splendors" in the kingdom.

With every encounter on every day we are presented an opportunity. Will we meet a person where they are and be Christ to them, or will we waste valuable time here on earth counting the cost, weighing the options, and determining whether or not they are indeed the neighbor we are called to love as ourselves? Here's the short answer: they are. They all are.

Of course, there are practical considerations and of course you must exercise prudence, but don't let your capacity to love be limited by overthinking. We have been created by God to do good works. Good works are to be "our way of life" (Ephesians 2:10). Opening our hearts in hospitality and mercy is the way of life of a Christian. Doing it with merriment—with honest joy—is the prayer of this study.

Elizabeth Foss

CONCENTRIC COMMUNITY CIRCLES

define your community

Use these suggestions to define your concentric community circles on the opposite page, but remember that each community is unique and that you may define yours differently.

1) INNER CIRCLE

family + close friends

People you interact with every day and share truth and vulnerability with.

keywords to describe this part of community:

love	closeness	other:
trust	intimate	
loyalty	reliable	
vulnerability	respect	

2) OUTER CIRCLE

distant family, friends, coworkers

People you interact with often and are comfortable with but not often vulnerable with.

keywords to describe this part of community:

friendly	caring	other:
understanding	trustworthy	
cordial		
polite		

3) OUTSIDE OF CIRCLES

distant family, friends, coworkers

People you interact with often and don't share truth with.

keywords to describe this part of community:

aquaintance	other:
unfamiliar	
distant	

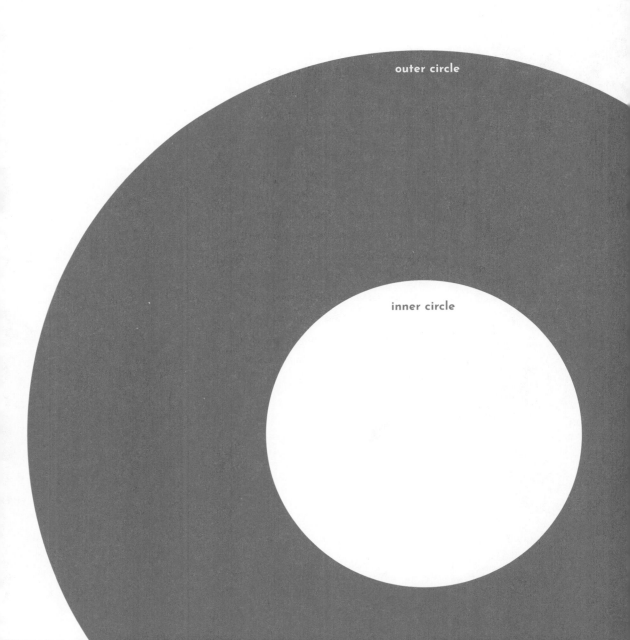

outside of circles

outer circle

inner circle

MATTHEW 25:32-40

All the nations will be gathered before him, and he will separate people one from another as a shepherd separates the sheep from the goats, and he will put the sheep at his right hand and the goats at the left. Then the king will say to those at his right hand, 'Come, you that are blessed by my Father, inherit the kingdom prepared for you from the foundation of the world; for I was hungry and you gave me food, I was thirsty and you gave me something to drink, I was a stranger and you welcomed me, I was naked and you gave me clothing, I was sick and you took care of me, I was in prison and you visited me.' Then the righteous will answer him, 'Lord, when was it that we saw you hungry and gave you food, or thirsty and gave you something to drink? And when was it that we saw you a stranger and welcomed you, or naked and gave you clothing? And when was it that we saw you sick or in prison and visited you?' And the king will answer them, 'Truly I tell you, just as you did it to one of the least of these who are members of my family, you did it to me.'

For further reading:
Hebrews 4:14-16
Matthew 7:12
2 Corinthians 1:3-4

Date:

REACH OUT   RESOLVE   REJOICE

How can you reach someone inside of your circles today?

How will you live out what God has shared with your heart in today's reading?

Count three blessings:

How can you reach outside of your circles today?

Ways I fostered community today: Prayer Intentions

- ○ prayed for a friend
- ○ put down my phone in the presence of people
- ○ made plans to host a gathering
- ○ replied "yes" to an invitation
- ○ hugged someone important to me
- ○ shared a meal with someone special
- ○ wrote a letter by hand
- ○ set a table for more than myself
- ○ introduced myself to someone new
- ○ made time for these people:

- ○ other:

Asking God's help for myself:

Day Four

She was fifteen years old and thirty-four weeks pregnant when she arrived at our pregnancy hostel to await the birth of her baby. She was quiet and her shy smile tentative. She carried a small purse that I knew contained only the identification documents she needed to be admitted to the hospital. As I showed her to her bed and gave her a quick layout of our pregnancy hostel for indigenous mothers in the Costa Rican mountains, I asked if she had any immediate needs I could help her with. She lowered her eyes and quietly asked if I had any underwear. To this day, I wonder at the courage it took for her to ask. Weeks later, she would go into labor one evening and pace outside as I watched her from the window. At the hospital, we'd wait outside to be called in and I would rub her lower back and hold her hand. She would tell me for the first time how scared she was, how her own mother had died giving birth to her little sister, how she was sure labor would kill her. She wouldn't tell me that her water had broken while we waited.

Her baby girl was one of the first I saw born after the hospital in Costa Rica started allowing me to stay with the mothers we served during their labors and deliveries. And I will ever carry Paola and her sweet Isabella with me in my heart. In the years that I was the administrator of our center, I served the needs of hundreds of women. I saw countless little ones enter the world, some accidentally into my own hands. And never once did I fail to see the wonder in the opportunity.

In our Westernized version of this parable of the sheep or the goats, we tend to train our eyes on the Christ-like nature of the ones doing the giving. The ones who feed the hungry and clothe the needy. They are so very like Christ. But in doing so, we have reversed the parable. Those who serve the needs of others are the sheep in the story. It is the ones in need who are like Christ.

Our God is a God of invitation. He comes to us needy, as he did literally when he took on human flesh in the world. Ever since then, in the flesh of our brothers and sisters, he invites us to meet him in that need. It is an act of humble courage on the part of our God to entrust himself to our keeping. We are fickle and riddled with imperfections that far too often make his vulnerability with us a risk not worth taking. Yet still he comes to us, weak and waiting, a baby in need of a place to be born, a body in need of a tomb to be laid in, a young pregnant girl in need of a hand to hold while she brings her daughter into the world. God constantly offers us the opportunity to behold the mystery of a God who needs nothing from us yet wants everything we have to offer. A God who loves for love's sake and presents himself to us in need so that we too may learn to love Love for love's sake.

To live a life of love of others is to realize that it is they who are being Christ-like to us when they risk being vulnerable, when they allow us to see their need, and when they graciously accept our imperfect attempts at meeting that need. To be a sheep is to know the voice of the shepherd and to follow his call, especially when his call is a call for help.

Colleen Connell

DEFINE YOUR SUPPORT SYSTEM

Take some time to define your support network, including whom you give support to. Try to think past your inner circle of intimate relationships and think broader and wider. Go beyond survival needs, like emergency situations, and also consider your daily emotional needs. Refer to your concentric community circles to review who makes up your community. After you've defined how your needs are supported, consider how you can support the needs of others.

Use the following questions and lists to fill out the support system on the next page:

Who can you call for emergencies?

Who can you call for friendly conversation?

Who can help you with home issues, like a leaky faucet or a broken garage door?

Who can join you for Mass once a week?

Who can talk about the Bible and your faith with you?

Who can accompany you on an outing?

Who can you invite over for dinner?

Who can you call when you're upset?

Who can help you fix a problem you've had for a long time?

Who can make you smile on a bad day?

What can you offer someone in need? What kinds of needs can you support?

PEOPLE + PLACES
you might __receive__ support from:

family members
spouse or significant other
close friends
coworkers
neighbors
church community
counselor or therapist
doctor
hired help
volunteer help

PEOPLE + PLACES
you might be able to __give__ support to:

family members
spouse or significant other
children, grandchildren, nieces, and nephews
close friends
coworkers
neighbors
church community
someone with less
someone who's sick
the lonely

* Refer to your concentric community circles on page 25 to review whom you share truth + vulnerability with. Most of these people will overlap in your support system.

COMMUNITY SUPPORT SYSTEM

How I receive support:

NEED	NAME	RELATION
1. Start your list of needs here:	2. Write down the names of people who can help support these needs:	3. What is your relationship with this person?

How I give support:

NAME	RELATION	SUPPORT
1. Start with naming a person you can aid in support:	2. What is your relationship with this person?	3. What kind of support are you able to give this person?

COLOSSIANS 3:12-17

As God's chosen ones, holy and beloved, clothe yourselves with compassion, kindness, humility, meekness, and patience. Bear with one another and, if anyone has a complaint against another, forgive each other; just as the Lord has forgiven you, so you also must forgive. Above all, clothe yourselves with love, which binds everything together in perfect harmony. And let the peace of Christ rule in your hearts, to which indeed you were called in the one body. And be thankful. Let the word of Christ dwell in you richly; teach and admonish one another in all wisdom; and with gratitude in your hearts sing psalms, hymns, and spiritual songs to God. And whatever you do, in word or deed, do everything in the name of the Lord Jesus, giving thanks to God the Father through him.

For further reading:
Psalm 133:1-3
1 John 1

REACH OUT   RESOLVE   REJOICE

How can you reach someone inside of your circles today?

How will you live out what God has shared with your heart in today's reading?

Count three blessings:

How can you reach outside of your circles today?

Ways I fostered community today: Prayer Intentions

○ **prayed for a friend**
○ **put down my phone in the presence of people**
○ **made plans to host a gathering**
○ **replied "yes" to an invitation**
○ **hugged someone important to me**
○ **shared a meal with someone special**
○ **wrote a letter by hand**
○ **set a table for more than myself**
○ **introduced myself to someone new**
○ **made time for these people:**

○ **other:**

Asking God's help for myself:

Day Five

I recently heard someone refer to close, nice friends as "low-lying fruit." I loved the image—people who are easy to love are, well, easy to love.

Isn't friendship a wonderful blessing! Being surrounded by people who love us is a blessed way to live life. And God wants us to have those friendships, to share life with people who draw us closer to him through their patience and kindness and steadfast faithfulness.

Loving is easy when it's someone easy to love.

But then we switch out the image of our best friends, those people who build us up and draw us closer to Jesus, and we insert someone a little different from us. Instead of someone who makes us feel good, it's someone who isn't that kind or patient or loving. Maybe it's even someone who is mean and rude.

Do I really have to love that person? we ask. Must I be patient and forgiving with them as well?

I read verses like this beautiful passage from Colossians, an exhortation to forgive and be patient and love, and I get chills. Yes, Lord! I want to be a saint! I want to love and exhort and focus on virtue and goodness. I want to be Jesus to those in my path!

And I know that in order to really do that, the way Jesus needs us to, we have to be willing to do this with everyone, the easy people and the difficult ones alike. That's the scary part—learning to love and live life with those who aren't so easy to be around.

Difficult people. I like to call them "saint-makers." They are the people not as easy to love, those who sometimes bring out the worst in us. Hurt people hurt people, and sometimes it takes a minute to remember that the prickly pear deserves just as much love and patience as the really wonderful person—maybe even more.

We have to learn to love not for what we get out of it (good feelings, knowing we are loved) but because it's what Jesus tells us to do. What he is telling us right here in this Scripture passage puts us on the path to holiness, and it's where real growth happens.

When we love the "unlovable," we get closer to being a saint. We act out of selflessness, operating not out of what's in it for us, but out of what Jesus can do in us and through us.

The key to living this kind of life, loving the low-lying fruit as well as that apple that seems impossibly out of reach, is to focus less on ourselves and more on Jesus.

We focus less on what makes someone nice or rude and we focus on Jesus. We love Jesus and experience his great love for us and somehow, mystically, through lots of hard work and no effort at all, we have the grace to give thanks to God the Father and to love his people. We are inspired to let Christ's peace permeate our souls and our lives and this gives us the strength we need to live life fully with those around us.

This kind of love yields true freedom because we love as Jesus loved us. Deeply. Fully. And with no strings attached.

Rachel Balducci

2 CORINTHIANS 9

Now it is not necessary for me to write you about the ministry to the saints, for I know your eagerness, which is the subject of my boasting about you to the people of Macedonia, saying that Achaia has been ready since last year; and your zeal has stirred up most of them. But I am sending the brothers in order that our boasting about you may not prove to have been empty in this case, so that you may be ready, as I said you would be; otherwise, if some Macedonians come with me and find that you are not ready, we would be humiliated—to say nothing of you—in this undertaking. So I thought it necessary to urge the brothers to go on ahead to you, and arrange in advance for this bountiful gift that you have promised, so that it may be ready as a voluntary gift and not as an extortion.

The point is this: the one who sows sparingly will also reap sparingly, and the one who sows bountifully will also reap bountifully. Each of you must give as you have made up your mind, not reluctantly or under compulsion, for God loves a cheerful giver. And God is able to provide you with every blessing in abundance, so that by always having enough of everything, you may share abundantly in every good work. As it is written,

"He scatters abroad, he gives to the
     poor;
  his righteousness endures forever."

He who supplies seed to the sower and bread for food will supply and multiply your seed for sowing and increase the harvest of your righteousness. You will be enriched in every way for your great generosity, which will produce thanksgiving to God through us; for the rendering of this ministry not only supplies the needs of the saints but also overflows with many thanksgivings to God. Through the testing of this ministry you glorify God by your obedience to the confession of the gospel of Christ and by the generosity of your sharing with them and with all others, while they long for you and pray for you because of the surpassing grace of God that he has given you. Thanks be to God for his indescribable gift!

For further reading:
Matthew 6:1-6

REACH OUT   RESOLVE   REJOICE

How can you reach someone inside of your circles today?

How will you live out what God has shared with your heart in today's reading?

Count three blessings:

How can you reach outside of your circles today?

Ways I fostered community today: Prayer Intentions

○ **prayed for a friend**
○ **put down my phone in the presence of people**
○ **made plans to host a gathering**
○ **replied "yes" to an invitation**
○ **hugged someone important to me**
○ **shared a meal with someone special**
○ **wrote a letter by hand**
○ **set a table for more than myself**
○ **introduced myself to someone new**
○ **made time for these people:**

○ **other:**

Asking God's help for myself:

Day Six

"So I thought it necessary to urge the brothers to go on ahead to you, and arrange in advance for this bountiful gift that you have promised, so that it may be ready as a voluntary gift and not as an extortion" (2 Corinthians 9:5). In other words, he told them, "I know y'all can cook, and you know how to throw a party, so you'd better get after it because we're heading your way."

Two thousand years later, I read his words and my instinct is to sigh with the exhaustion that seems to infect our whole society, and I think, "I'm too tired for this nonsense. Who has the time or the extra money to throw an impromptu party?" St. Paul isn't even writing to me, and I'm too tired to even think of feeding the people he brought home to dinner two thousand years ago. The more I thought on it, the more I wondered—am I really too tired and busy, or am I just making this all harder than it really needs to be?

Back when I was a young woman and a new bride, my husband and I often joined his grandmother for the potluck dinners her church held once a month in their hall. The congregation was made up of farmers and small-town people, and it was in the days before Pinterest turned us all into wannabe overachievers, so the food was simple, filling, and plentiful. If you walked out of that room hungry, it was by your own choice and because you'd somehow managed to avoid the serving ladies who brought around seconds, thirds, and more until you threw your paper plate away.

Those potluck dinners weren't fancy at all. They hadn't set out to impress anyone. They were just welcoming and warm, and they made that small country church feel like home to anyone fortunate enough to be there that afternoon. To a girl eight hundred miles from family, aching with loneliness, those overfilled plates and homemade dishes were echoes of home and were everywhere that I wanted to be.

They were exactly the type of warm reception that I think St. Paul was talking about when he wrote that he was bringing people and the congregation's readiness should be "a voluntary gift and not as an extortion." He gave them lots of warning, and ample time to spread work around. He didn't call for impressive; he called for warmth and welcome, and an invitation to join in the community of believers.

St. Paul probably didn't know he was talking about cold ham, scalloped potatoes, and Jell-O salad when he wrote to his followers way back then, but the church table that groaned under the weight of all that food in Enid, Oklahoma, the work of so many hands, was probably exactly the kind of thing that he had in mind.

We live in a time that says things have to be bigger and better, cooler and more fun, and definitely anything we pull together has to be Pinterest and social media ready. It's not about the hospitality any more, but about how great things look to all the people who weren't there. The simple, unfussy potluck dinners from Grandma's church seem like relics of the past and not a big enough production for today. But there was an honesty and an ease to those potluck dinners that Pinterest cannot capture.

St. Paul is writing to us just as much as he was writing to the Christians in his own time. He is calling on us to make welcome the people who are being sent to us, to welcome the travelers, the strangers, and those without a people. We don't have to make it fancy; in fact, it's probably better if it's not. He's telling us to break bread with each other and to sow our efforts generously. We never know what seeds we may be planting in someone else's heart over store-bought rolls, a mess of chicken, and an ice-box pie; but he tells us that if we do it cheerfully, the harvest will be an abundant one.

Rebecca Frech

Selah

Selah is a Hebrew word found often in the psalms and a few times in Habakkuk. Scholars aren't absolutely certain what it means. It seems to be a musical or liturgical note—maybe a pause or crescendo.

We have set aside this space—this day—for you to use as your selah. Perhaps you pause here and just review what you have pondered thus far. Perhaps you rejoice here and use the space for shouts of praise. Or maybe you take the opportunity to fill in some gaps in the pages before this one.

It's your space.

Selah.

Give it meaning.

Check in.

TODAY'S DATE	PLACE OF PEACE:
_____ | ___| ___	_____

I'M FEELING

- ○ happy
- ○ excited
- ○ joyful

- ○ anxious
- ○ lonely
- ○ tired

- ○ connected
- ○ angry
- ○ sad

- ○ grateful
- ○ confused
- ○ peaceful

- ○ _____
- ○ _____
- ○ _____

In my community:	Working on my heart:
Missed connections + opportunities for togetherness:	**Listening to:**
	In my prayers:
Giving thanks for:	**Hope for next week:**

MILK BOTTLE TUTORIAL

a simple way to make welcome

Try this easy tutorial at home to make custom, bright vases for your next gathering. If you don't have mini milk bottles on hand, use any small glass bottles you have to create an eclectic mix of vases.

You will need:
- mini milk bottles or small glass vases
- spray paint for glass
- *anything you might dream up to put in your vases, or take a peek at our suggested bottle recipes!*

1) Step one

Prep + clean

Prep the space you will be painting in, whether it's laying down a paint drop cloth or some newspaper.

Clean the mini milk jugs with soap and water. Make sure that the glass is dry and dust free before painting.

2) Step two

Spray + allow to dry

Follow the directions on the spray paint can and spray a thorough coat of paint on the mini milk jugs. Make sure you are in a well-ventilated area for safety and to allow the paint to dry.

Apply a second coat if needed and allow to dry.

3) Step three

Decorate + have fun

Decorate your vases for your next gathering or take some ideas from the next page.

RECIPES FOR MILK JUGS

Use these combinations to create simple centerpieces for any occasion!

sunny day

Vase color: sunny yellow
Decorate with: sky blue
ribbon
Add: white daisies, or your
favorite summer flower

backyard bouquet

Vase color: white and pink
stripes
Decorate with: try adding
stripes with painter's tape
Add: anything that's easy to
find in your backyard or a
safe nearby wooded area

creative collective

Vase color: rainbow
Decorate with: glitter
Add: coloring pencils or
paint brushes and host an
art night

fruitful

Vase color: your pick
Decorate with: hand
lettering
Add: fruit kabobs

Praying Together

KEEP

yourselves

IN THE

love of
God

Praying Together

SCRIPTURE MEMORY

But you, beloved, build yourselves up on your most holy faith; pray in the Holy Spirit; keep yourselves in the love of God; look forward to the mercy of our Lord Jesus Christ that leads to eternal life.

JUDE 1:20-21

I will practice Scripture memory by

- ○ Praying
- ○ Writing
- ○ Speaking
- ○ Reading
- ○ Other: _____

BAKED ZITI

Ingredients

- ◯ 1 pound ziti noodles (you can substitute penne)

- ◯ 1½ pounds ground sweet Italian sausage

- ◯ 5 cloves garlic, minced

- ◯ 1 (28-oz) can crushed tomatoes

- ◯ 1 teaspoon salt

- ◯ ¼ teaspoon crushed red pepper flakes

- ◯ 1 cup whole milk ricotta cheese

- ◯ ½ cup grated Parmesan cheese

- ◯ ⅓ cup chopped fresh basil, plus more for serving

- ◯ 8 ounces whole milk mozzarella cheese, shredded (about 2 cups)

When I make baked ziti, I make two. These freeze beautifully, and it's nice to have one in the freezer to be able to bring a friend on a moment's notice.

Directions

Preheat the oven to 425°F and set the oven rack in the middle position.

Bring a large pot of salted water to a boil. Cook the ziti according to the package directions for very al dente, about 7 minutes. (Because it will continue to cook in the oven, you want it slightly undercooked.) Drain and add the pasta back to the pot. Set aside.

While the pot is boiling, heat a large iron skillet over medium-high heat. Crumble the sausage into the pan and cook, breaking apart with a wooden spoon, until just cooked through, 5 to 6 minutes. Use a slotted spoon to transfer the cooked sausage to a large bowl.

Drain all but 1 tablespoon of the fat from the pan and set over low heat. If you don't have enough fat to coat the pan, add a tablespoon of olive oil. Add the garlic and just let it sizzle. Be careful not to brown it or it will become bitter. Add the crushed tomatoes, salt, and red pepper flakes and simmer, uncovered, for 10 minutes.

Combine the ricotta, $1/3$ cup of the Parmesan, and basil to the bowl with the crumbled sausage. Stir until well combined.

Carefully pour the contents of the sauté pan into the large pot with the pasta and gently stir to combine. Then, add the sausage and ricotta mixture, gently folding until all is combined evenly.

Spoon half of the mixture into a 9 x 13-inch baking dish. Sprinkle with half of the shredded mozzarella and half of the remaining Parmesan cheese. Spoon the remaining pasta mixture on top and sprinkle with the remaining mozzarella and Parmesan. Transfer to the oven and bake, uncovered, until the cheese has melted and browned, 15 to 20 minutes.

Sprinkle with more basil and serve.

Make Ahead: This dish can be assembled and refrigerated, tightly covered with foil, up to 2 days in advance. Since the dish will be cold, the baking time will need to be increased. Bake, still covered tightly with aluminum foil, in a 425°F oven for 25 minutes. Then uncover and bake for another 10 to 15 minutes or until the cheese is lightly browned and the pasta is hot throughout.

Freezer-Friendly Instructions: The dish can be frozen unbaked. Cover tightly with foil and freeze. When you're ready to cook it, defrost in the refrigerator for 24 hours, then proceed with the Make Ahead instructions above.

MATTHEW 18:19-20

"Again, truly I tell you, if two of you agree on earth about anything you ask, it will be done for you by my Father in heaven. For where two or three are gathered in my name, I am there among them."

For further reading:
2 Corinthians 1:24
Luke 9:28
Acts 4:31

REACH OUT   RESOLVE   REJOICE

How can you reach someone inside of your circles today?

How will you live out what God has shared with your heart in today's reading?

Count three blessings:

How can you reach outside of your circles today?

Ways I fostered community today: Prayer Intentions

- ○ prayed for a friend
- ○ put down my phone in the presence of people
- ○ made plans to host a gathering
- ○ replied "yes" to an invitation
- ○ hugged someone important to me
- ○ shared a meal with someone special
- ○ wrote a letter by hand
- ○ set a table for more than myself
- ○ introduced myself to someone new
- ○ made time for these people:

- ○ other:

Asking God's help for myself:

Day Nine

It took me days to work up the courage to call her, but I knew I needed her wisdom, and when I finally reached the end of myself, I poured it all out to my friend and mentor. She listened intently, never interrupting but occasionally asking a clarifying question. When I finished in a grateful rush, I took a deep breath and wiped tears from my cheeks. Her first words at once surprised me and poured over me like the sweetest kindness I've ever known.

"Can I pray for you right now? The two of us? Can we bow our heads together and ask God into our conversation?"

It does not happen often in my faith tradition. Two or more gathered in prayer outside of structured occasions for prayer is not a typical scenario. But when it does happen, it's a long exhale into the grace of God. Our Lord intends for us to invite him into our communities intentionally. Prayer is a beautiful gift—the God of the universe inclining his ear to hear our hearts—and the joy of the gift is multiplied when we share it with others.

Prayer is a channel for the fruits of the Spirit. God wants us to have love, joy, peace, patience, kindness, goodness, faithfulness, and self-control. Asking for them in prayer opens us to his gift of the fruits. When we're gathered together with others to ask, we receive them, but so do the people who are praying with us. Prayer benefits all those who are gathered to pray. Asking someone if you can pray with her is asking to be an instrument by which God can multiply his gifts for her. We come together in prayer with confidence that we increase the joy of everyone in the community gathered. And when we multiply our joy, we multiply his glory!

To pray with another person, or even a small group, is to make ourselves vulnerable. Our personal conversations with God are intimate, and prayer in a pair or in a small group loses the anonymity afforded by large corporate liturgies. The facades are peeled away, and hearts are laid bare. An interesting benefit of this vulnerability is the opportunity to better understand the people with whom we're praying. Friendships are knit more securely when we see that the people gathered have a relationship with our Father too. There is kinship in prayer; we are more tightly bound as a family when we pray together.

It is relatively easy for me to awaken in the morning and give over the first half hour of my day to prayer. Even if my children interrupt my solitary prayer pursuits, I can keep a running dialogue with Christ inside my head as I scramble eggs and pour coffee and check the dryer for a missing sock. Praying with a small group requires more intention. We have to synchronize schedules and find a place suitable for spoken words lifted heavenward. Perhaps more difficult, we have to give consent to laying our souls bare and letting someone else see our most intimate relationship. God calls us to do exactly that and he offers us beautiful rewards when we do.

Praying with someone else helps us know that friend better, but perhaps the greatest gift is that it helps us know Jesus better. In each of us are God's image and likeness, and in every soul, the spark of the divine. What is truly extraordinary is that every unique person shows us another facet of our Lord. To pray with someone—to open your soul to her conversation as well as God's—is to see the Creator in her. God promises that what you ask will be done. This gives us pause and makes us wonder. Even more, he assures you that if you pray together, he will show up for it. That is the most compelling reason of all to gather in his name.

Elizabeth Foss

JAMES 5:13-16

Are any among you suffering? They should pray. Are any cheerful? They should sing songs of praise. Are any among you sick? They should call for the elders of the church and have them pray over them, anointing them with oil in the name of the Lord. The prayer of faith will save the sick, and the Lord will raise them up; and anyone who has committed sins will be forgiven. Therefore confess your sins to one another, and pray for one another, so that you may be healed. The prayer of the righteous is powerful and effective.

For further reading:
Mark 6:6-13
Acts 5:12-16

REACH OUT

RESOLVE

REJOICE

How can you reach someone inside of your circles today?

How will you live out what God has shared with your heart in today's reading?

Count three blessings:

How can you reach outside of your circles today?

Ways I fostered community today:

Prayer Intentions

- ○ prayed for a friend
- ○ put down my phone in the presence of people
- ○ made plans to host a gathering
- ○ replied "yes" to an invitation
- ○ hugged someone important to me
- ○ shared a meal with someone special
- ○ wrote a letter by hand
- ○ set a table for more than myself
- ○ introduced myself to someone new
- ○ made time for these people:

- ○ other:

Asking God's help for myself:

Day Ten

Personal prayer is critical to grow and maintain our relationship with God, but as we're reminded by St. James, we are called to pray for each other as a community too. Where two or more are gathered in his name, God is there—communal prayer not only bonds and links us; it is also powerful.

A few days after I had my first high-risk surgery, I found out that just as it was beginning, several high school students from our church's youth ministry program had left their classes, gathered in the school hallway, and prayed for me. I was incredibly touched that they'd thought of me and taken the time to gather together for my sake. Hearing of their prayers boosted my morale and helped me face a difficult recovery.

Several weeks later, I was only partly through what would be many more months of medical treatment, but I was well enough to return to our church. After Mass, I ran into one of the students who'd prayed for me. She immediately began apologizing and said that she was so disappointed that their prayers hadn't worked, since I hadn't been completely and miraculously healed. I was so surprised by her apology that I merely hugged her and tried to express how much her kindness meant to me, no matter the outcome for my health.

Yet I wish I had told her that the strongest memory I had of that frightening day was how my fear faded away and how, instead, a surprising sense of peace overcame me. I know that this was through no merit of my own, and I can only understand it as a gift of God's grace. So while it's true that those students' prayers didn't result in my complete and miraculous healing, they did lift me up, if only in a different way than they'd imagined.

We often don't see the effect that our prayers have on the lives of others. And in many cases, those effects look totally different than we expect or want them to look. Because God's ways are not our ways; they are always more imaginative and always perfect. Sometimes, it seems that our prayers have no effect at all. God's answer might be to wait for whatever healing or fulfillment is yearned for, or the answer might simply be no, at least not this side of heaven. We won't always see physical healing when we pray for it for ourselves or for those who are sick, and we won't always see an end to suffering when we beg God for it. And that can break our hearts and make it difficult to keep hoping and praying.

But Scripture tells us that God has a plan for our lives, and that prayer changes things. While those things may seem contradictory, they only are if we think that prayer is about changing God's mind. If prayer is instead about honestly bringing our hopes and needs to God, and about learning to align our will with his as much as possible, there's no contradiction at all.

As members of the body of Christ joined together, God invites us to participate in his plan of salvation—to become coworkers with him in an amazing way. Sometimes we will see the healing we pray for occur, because that was God's will, and our prayers played a part in fulfilling that will. It is an incredible gift and testament to faith when that happens. But it's perhaps an even greater testament to our faith when that doesn't happen, and we continue to trust that God always hears us and that he is always working things for the good of his children anyway.

God is there when we gather and pray together, and that prayer strengthens the faith of each person praying as well as the faith of the entire body of Christ. When we intercede through prayer for one another to our God, we grow as a community in compassion and practice selfless love towards our brothers and sisters. This draws the entire Church closer to Christ and helps spur us to act as his hands and feet to our community in the Church, as well as to the greater community of the world.

Allison McGinley

ACTS 12:1-17

About that time King Herod laid violent hands upon some who belonged to the church. He had James, the brother of John, killed with the sword. After he saw that it pleased the Jews, he proceeded to arrest Peter also. (This was during the festival of Unleavened Bread.) When he had seized him, he put him in prison and handed him over to four squads of soldiers to guard him, intending to bring him out to the people after the Passover. While Peter was kept in prison, the church prayed fervently to God for him.

The very night before Herod was going to bring him out, Peter, bound with two chains, was sleeping between two soldiers, while guards in front of the door were keeping watch over the prison. Suddenly an angel of the Lord appeared and a light shone in the cell. He tapped Peter on the side and woke him, saying, "Get up quickly." And the chains fell off his wrists. The angel said to him, "Fasten your belt and put on your sandals." He did so. Then he said to him, "Wrap your cloak around you and follow me." Peter went out and followed him; he did not realize that what was happening with the angel's help was real; he thought he was seeing a vision. After they had passed the first and the second guard, they came before the iron gate leading into the city. It opened for them of its own accord, and they went outside and walked along a lane, when suddenly the angel left him. Then Peter came to himself and said, "Now I am sure that the Lord has sent his angel and rescued me from the hands of Herod and from all that the Jewish people were expecting."

As soon as he realized this, he went to the house of Mary, the mother of John whose other name was Mark, where many had gathered and were praying. When he knocked at the outer gate, a maid named Rhoda came to answer. On recognizing Peter's voice, she was so overjoyed that, instead of opening the gate, she ran in and announced that Peter was standing at the gate. They said to her, "You are out of your mind!" But she insisted that it was so. They said, "It is his angel." Meanwhile Peter continued knocking; and when they opened the gate, they saw him and were amazed. He motioned to them with his hand to be silent, and described for them how the Lord had brought him out of the prison. And he added, "Tell this to James and to the believers." Then he left and went to another place.

For further reading:
1 Corinthians 1:3-4
Philippians 2:1-30

REACH OUT   RESOLVE   REJOICE

How can you reach someone inside of your circles today?

How will you live out what God has shared with your heart in today's reading?

Count three blessings:

How can you reach outside of your circles today?

Ways I fostered community today: Prayer Intentions

- ○ prayed for a friend
- ○ put down my phone in the presence of people
- ○ made plans to host a gathering
- ○ replied "yes" to an invitation
- ○ hugged someone important to me
- ○ shared a meal with someone special
- ○ wrote a letter by hand
- ○ set a table for more than myself
- ○ introduced myself to someone new
- ○ made time for these people:

- ○ other:

Asking God's help for myself:

How many times has my phone beeped, often late at night, with a prayer request? My baby is sick with an awful fever. Will you pray? My husband is out of a job. Please ask St. Joseph to pray for us. My mom's cancer is back. I'm too scared to pray. Will you do it for me?

Never in my life, though, have I received a message with the gravitas of what was probably passed between the apostles and other early members of the Church.

"James was martyred, beheaded by Herod. Peter is next in line, waiting in prison. Please ask everyone to pray."

In Acts 12:5, St. Luke says, "While Peter was kept in prison, the church prayed fervently to God for him." This was Peter's third imprisonment, but James was the first martyred apostle, and it must have shaken them all deeply.

The next verses tell us of one of Scripture's most wildly exciting rescues. An angel awakens the imprisoned Peter, unchains him, whisks him past guards, gates, and sentries. The moment is so surreal that it isn't until the angel disappears that Peter understands that it wasn't all a dream or a vision.

I'd hazard a guess that many a fiction writer wishes he had dreamed up this escape first. But no, it was a God original, an answer to the heartfelt pleas of the Church on Peter's behalf.

The *Catechism of the Catholic Church* tells us more about intercessory prayer in paragraphs 2634–2636. Specifically, in *CCC*, 2636, we learn about its role in the life of the early Church:

> The first Christian communities lived this form of fellowship intensely. Thus the Apostle Paul gives them a share in his ministry of preaching the Gospel but also intercedes for them. The intercession of Christians recognizes no boundaries.

Not only did the Lord hear the prayers of the early Church on Peter's behalf, but he answered them in a lavish, miraculous way. Of course, God does not answer all of our prayers in such a way. Oftentimes he answers them in ways we rather wish he didn't or so quietly and humbly that we forget to thank him—and our intercessors—at all.

But Peter does not forget. He recognizes the Lord's role through his angel, and then immediately seeks his friends.

Of course he does! He's just experienced a miraculous deliverance during the feast of Unleavened Bread, a rescue that echoes Israel's escape from captivity in Egypt after the first Passover. Peter can't wait to tell his dearest companions, who he surely knew were praying for him.

Isn't Rhoda's response motion picture worthy? In her surprise and eagerness, she runs inside to tell the others, forgetting to let Peter in the gate. How wonderfully precious is it that she is as excited and forgetful as one of us might be? Through Rhoda, the human response to an answered prayer echoes down the ages.

But behind that locked gate, inside St. Mark's mother's home, Peter hears his friends' incredulous responses. They were more ready to believe that Rhoda had gone mad or that Peter's angel was at the door than that the Lord had delivered Peter.

How do you respond when Christ answers your prayers or those of your friends on your behalf? Who are you most like in this stranger-than-fiction story?

Are you like Peter? Do you rush to your friends, knock on their door in the dead of night, to share the indulgent love of God and your thanksgiving to him who is all good?

Are you Rhoda, who in her excitement at an answered prayer runs to share it with the Church? Do you proclaim the miracles—great and small—to everyone around you?

Or are you, perhaps, more like the people inside the house, who call those proclaiming miracles crazy? Are you willing to offer prayers but skeptical of the results?

I have said before that St. Peter is my favorite knucklehead. But that was Gospel Peter, Pre-Pentecost Peter. The Peter here in Acts, infused with the Holy Spirit, knows Jesus is calling him to teach and serve his community, possibly to die for them as well, and he does it willingly, with thanks to God and to the family of believers who surround him with their prayers.

Micaela Darr

LUKE 22:7-30

Then came the day of Unleavened Bread, on which the Passover lamb had to be sacrificed. So Jesus sent Peter and John, saying, "Go and prepare the Passover meal for us that we may eat it." They asked him, "Where do you want us to make preparations for it?" "Listen," he said to them, "when you have entered the city, a man carrying a jar of water will meet you; follow him into the house he enters and say to the owner of the house, 'The teacher asks you, "Where is the guest room, where I may eat the Passover with my disciples?"' He will show you a large room upstairs, already furnished. Make preparations for us there." So they went and found everything as he had told them; and they prepared the Passover meal. When the hour came, he took his place at the table, and the apostles with him. He said to them, "I have eagerly desired to eat this Passover with you before I suffer; for I tell you, I will not eat it until it is fulfilled in the kingdom of God." Then he took a cup, and after giving thanks he said, "Take this and divide it among yourselves; for I tell you that from now on I will not drink of the fruit of the vine until the kingdom of God comes." Then he took a loaf of bread, and when he had given thanks, he broke it and gave it to them, saying, "This is my body, which is given for you. Do this in remembrance of me." And he did the same with the cup after supper, saying,

"This cup that is poured out for you is the new covenant in my blood. But see, the one who betrays me is with me, and his hand is on the table. For the Son of Man is going as it has been determined, but woe to that one by whom he is betrayed!" Then they began to ask one another which one of them it could be who would do this. A dispute also arose among them as to which one of them was to be regarded as the greatest. But he said to them, "The kings of the Gentiles lord it over them; and those in authority over them are called benefactors. But not so with you; rather the greatest among you must become like the youngest, and the leader like one who serves. For who is greater, the one who is at the table or the one who serves? Is it not the one at the table? But I am among you as one who serves.

"You are those who have stood by me in my trials; and I confer on you, just as my Father has conferred on me, a kingdom, so that you may eat and drink at my table in my kingdom, and you will sit on thrones judging the twelve tribes of Israel."

For further reading:
1 Corinthians 11:17-34

REACH OUT   RESOLVE   REJOICE

How can you reach someone inside of your circles today?

How will you live out what God has shared with your heart in today's reading?

Count three blessings:

How can you reach outside of your circles today?

Ways I fostered community today: Prayer Intentions

- ○ prayed for a friend
- ○ put down my phone in the presence of people
- ○ made plans to host a gathering
- ○ replied "yes" to an invitation
- ○ hugged someone important to me
- ○ shared a meal with someone special
- ○ wrote a letter by hand
- ○ set a table for more than myself
- ○ introduced myself to someone new
- ○ made time for these people:

- ○ other:

Asking God's help for myself:

Day Twelve

I grew up in a large Catholic family, and through all of our ups and downs, dinner together was a constant source of comfort and connection. The family table shaped me so much it led me to food blogging and cultivating the tradition in my own family so that we've come to cherish dinnertime as the heartbeat of our days. We are nourished by it through so much more than just food.

My Catholic faith and belief in the Eucharist no doubt led me to this deep reverence for family dinner. When I was in my twenties, our parish had twenty-four-hour Adoration, and I seemed to always get the middle of the night slots. In the wee hours were some of the richest spiritual deposits for me, thanks to reading meditations from Scripture on the Eucharist. My eyes were opened to the faithfulness and love in God's plan: the beautiful symmetry of the Old Testament when he fed his people manna from heaven while they were lost in the desert, and the new covenant Jesus made with us when he feeds us himself. In the old, God's mercy shone through sacrificing a pure lamb to atone for sin, and in the new, Jesus became that pure lamb, radiating mercy. It was like listening to a choir in harmony, like looking at a painting by a master. There was just so much beauty in it all.

But here's the thing: you don't need to be a cradle Catholic or go to Adoration in the middle of the night to be drawn towards it. Christ calls people to him through the Eucharist in all different ways. My husband thought hard about becoming a Catholic as we dated, and when he decided, he just said, "It's the Eucharist. That's what pulls me." Many conversion stories share a similar account, and they always deepen my faith.

When we read St. Luke's account of the Last Supper, this symmetry with the Old Testament is found in the first sentence, in the setting of the event itself: "Then came the day of Unleavened Bread, on which the Passover lamb had to be sacrificed." And then it details Jesus' plans, which sound for all the world like a bridegroom planning a wedding. "Find a man who will show you a large room upstairs, all furnished. Make preparations there." Like a groom to his bride, he tells his disciples, "I have eagerly desired to eat this Passover with you," and he speaks the sacred words, "This is my body given for you." God's plan all along was for the Church to be Christ's bride through the Eucharist.

Like many weddings, there was a lot of drama. There were disputes about who was the most important. Jesus used this conflict to make clear his desire for his disciples, his priests, to be ready to pour themselves out for the Church like he was. They should be like servants. Like husbands. And there was the one who wanted to thwart it all from happening, the devil, who planted seeds in Judas to betray Jesus, just as he tries to ruin priests and marriages today.

But in the middle of our human mess, in the simple act of eating and drinking, he prepares and edifies his disciples to build his Church. And he continues to do it with us. Communion with Christ is a love like a marriage, and as we grow devoted to him in an ever-deepening conversion, we find that the way to grow in holiness is to ask him to grow in us.

When we return to the world after Communion, we are changed. The graces that flow from it slowly transform us to be Christ-like. What if we imitate him, and follow his example of what he did at the Last Supper? If we say to our parents, cousins, nieces, and neighbors, "I have eagerly desired to eat with you," which might just sound like, "let's get together for pizza"? By opening up our hearts and breaking bread with people we are performing the simplest of acts, but as Christ showed us, it's a radical act of love that can change the world.

Katie Curtis

1 PETER 2:1-10

Rid yourselves, therefore, of all malice, and all guile, insincerity, envy, and all slander. Like newborn infants, long for the pure, spiritual milk, so that by it you may grow into salvation—if indeed you have tasted that the Lord is good.

Come to him, a living stone, though rejected by mortals yet chosen and precious in God's sight, and like living stones, let yourselves be built into a spiritual house, to be a holy priesthood, to offer spiritual sacrifices acceptable to God through Jesus Christ. For it stands in scripture:

> "See, I am laying in Zion a stone,
>   a cornerstone chosen and precious;
> and whoever believes in him will not
>   be put to shame."

To you then who believe, he is precious; but for those who do not believe,

> "The stone that the builders rejected
>   has become the very head of the
>   corner,"

and

> "A stone that makes them stumble,
>   and a rock that makes them fall."

They stumble because they disobey the word, as they were destined to do. But you are a chosen race, a royal priesthood, a holy nation, God's own people, in order that you may proclaim the mighty acts of him who called you out of darkness into his marvelous light.

> Once you were not a people,
>   but now you are God's people;
> once you had not received mercy,
>   but now you have received mercy.

MARK 6:6-7

Then he went about among the villages teaching. He called the twelve and began to send them out two by two, and gave them authority over the unclean spirits.

LUKE 10:1

After this the Lord appointed seventy others and sent them on ahead of him in pairs to every town and place where he himself intended to go.

For further reading:
1 Peter 3
2 Timothy 2:2
Ecclesiastes 4:9-12

REACH OUT   RESOLVE   REJOICE

How can you reach someone inside of your circles today?

How will you live out what God has shared with your heart in today's reading?

Count three blessings:

How can you reach outside of your circles today?

Ways I fostered community today: Prayer Intentions

- ○ prayed for a friend
- ○ put down my phone in the presence of people
- ○ made plans to host a gathering
- ○ replied "yes" to an invitation
- ○ hugged someone important to me
- ○ shared a meal with someone special
- ○ wrote a letter by hand
- ○ set a table for more than myself
- ○ introduced myself to someone new
- ○ made time for these people:

- ○ other:

Asking God's help for myself:

Day Thirteen

Recently, I sat with a friend who was shaken to her core after attending a school board meeting that was open to the public in order to discuss a contentious new policy. She went to be heard. A Christian mother of four small children, she wanted the school board to know her dearly held biblical worldview and how critical it is to how she and her husband are raising their children.

When people who were concerned about an assault on these values rose to speak, they were met with booing and hissing on the part of the proponents of the change. There were public shouts of outrage, and the people who were defending the gospel were called bigots and accused of spewing intolerance and hate. It was an ugly, ugly scene. When it was over, my friend made it to her van and burst into tears. She said she was determined to get to the car before crying because she didn't want her picture in the paper with a caption that characterized her as a hysterical Christian bigot.

She needed to talk that night. But our conversation actually lasted for days afterwards. It continues even on the day I write this essay. In the face of hostility—genuine persecution for gospel beliefs—she reached out for community.

We need each other. We cannot wait for Donut Sunday. We cannot limit ourselves to reaching behind us once a week to extend the sign of peace. We are called and commissioned by God himself to be Christ to one another and to gather as his own people to live in our calling as "a chosen race, a royal priesthood, a holy nation" (1 Peter 2:9).

We are "not ashamed of the gospel" (Romans 1:16) and we are called—all of us—to "have unity of spirit, sympathy, love for one another, a tender heart, and a humble mind" (1 Peter 3:8).

Jesus sent his disciples out in pairs. He knew we would need each other.

Community makes us more like Jesus. When we live in relationship with one another— especially when we pray with and for each other—we encourage and refine each other. In community, we are able to support and uphold each other practically, to actually carry one another's burdens. In the process of meeting practical needs, we learn a great deal about love.

Similarly, as a community of believers in the truth of the gospel, we are called to work through divisions amongst ourselves with grace. God wants unity, and it is possible, but it's not easy. Together, working from a place of truth in what Christ teaches about understanding one another and repenting and forgiving, the Christian community seeks unity with one another. That unity is a stronghold when they are confronted with anything contrary to Christ's plan for this world. Our awkwardness and messiness with one another are opportunities to grow in grace and to strengthen the skills we need to take on the formidable forces of a culture hostile to Christ. We can share light with a dark world because our brothers and sisters in Christ shine their lights into our own dark places.

The stone the builders discarded is now the cornerstone. Christ is the foundation of the life we build together. For those who don't trust him, the stone is in the way; they stumble over it. For those who do trust him, life is built around the stone. One by one, each together, we build upon the foundation he laid. None of us can do it alone. All of us can do it together.

Elizabeth Foss

Selah

Selah is a Hebrew word found often in the psalms and a few times in Habakkuk. Scholars aren't absolutely certain what it means. It seems to be a musical or liturgical note—maybe a pause or crescendo.

We have set aside this space—this day—for you to use as your selah. Perhaps you pause here and just review what you have pondered thus far. Perhaps you rejoice here and use the space for shouts of praise. Or maybe you take the opportunity to fill in some gaps in the pages before this one.

It's your space.

Selah.

Give it meaning.

Check in.

<table>
<tr><td>TODAY'S DATE</td><td>PLACE OF PEACE:</td></tr>
<tr><td>___ | ___ | ___</td><td>_____</td></tr>
</table>

I'M FEELING

○ happy   ○ anxious   ○ connected   ○ grateful   ○ _____

○ excited   ○ lonely   ○ angry   ○ confused   ○ _____

○ joyful   ○ tired   ○ sad   ○ peaceful   ○ _____

In my community:

Working on my heart:

Missed connections
+ opportunities for
togetherness:

Listening to:

In my prayers:

Giving thanks for:

Hope for next week:

Grace Before Meals

When we were engaged, a mentoring couple challenged my husband and me to identify the habits and traditions in each other's families of origin that we wanted to carry with us when we established our own family. The first thing Mike named was "Grace Before Meals."

I'm so glad.

I cannot imagine a family dinner without this deliberate pause to give thanks. "Grace" is rooted in the Latin word *gratia*, which means "thanksgiving." There is something so right and good about inhaling before we eat, thanking the Lord who created it all and asking his blessing on our gathering.

Around the table, we echo the prayers of the early Church—those disciples of our Lord whose gatherings are chronicled in the Book of Acts and teach us so much about being together. We breathe in the richness of food that will nourish body and soul, and we exhale gratitude.

Elizabeth Foss

Bless us,
O Lord,
and these, Thy gifts,
which we are about
to receive from
Thy bounty.
Through Christ,
our Lord.
Amen.

Making Welcome

serve

ONE

another

Making Welcome

SCRIPTURE MEMORY

Be hospitable to one another without complaining. Like good stewards of the manifold grace of God, serve one another with whatever gift each of you has received.

1 PETER 4:9-10

I will practice Scripture memory by
- ○ Praying
- ○ Writing
- ○ Speaking
- ○ Reading
- ○ Other: _____

FIESTA SALAD

Ingredients for the salad

- ○ 2 ears fresh corn or a small bag frozen corn
- ○ 1 cup chopped red onion
- ○ 1 (14.5 ounce) can black or kidney beans, rinsed well and drained
- ○ 1 red bell pepper, diced (about 1 cup)
- ○ ½ cup loosely packed fresh cilantro, chopped (save some for garnish)
- ○ 2 avocados
- ○ Juice of ½ fresh lime for finishing
- ○ Freshly ground pepper for finishing

Ingredients for the dressing

- ○ 2 tablespoons red wine vinegar
- ○ 2 tablespoons fresh lime juice, from 1-2 limes
- ○ 1 tablespoon honey
- ○ ⅓ cup good quality olive oil or avocado oil
- ○ 1 large garlic clove, minced
- ○ ¾ teaspoon cumin
- ○ ¾ teaspoon salt
- ○ ¼ teaspoon black pepper
- ○ 2 chipotle peppers in adobo sauce (These come in small cans; save the rest of the peppers and the sauce to season something else or to make this again tomorrow!)

This salad happened one May afternoon when I needed something to bring to a church picnic. We loved it so much that it became the go-to of the summer: lunch at the pool, a dip with tortilla chips while watching baseball on TV, and a main dish supper served over mixed greens. It works for whatever the occasion!

Directions

If you are using frozen corn, just let it thaw in a large bowl while you chop vegetables, and skip the rest of this step and the next step.

Bring a large pot of salted water to a boil. Add the corn, cover, and turn the heat down to low. Simmer for 8 minutes. Remove the corn from the water and rinse under cold water until it is cool.

Holding the cooled corn upright in a large bowl, cut the kernels off the cob in strips with a sharp knife.

Add the beans, red onion, red bell pepper, and cilantro to the bowl with the corn. Toss gently to combine.

Make the dressing by combining all of the ingredients in a blender, processing until smooth.

Pour the dressing over the salad and toss well. Cover and refrigerate for about 1 hour. If you don't have an hour, it's fine.

Right before serving, slice the avocados in half. Remove the pits and cut the flesh into cubes. Holding the avocado halves over the salad, gently scoop out the diced flesh with a spoon. Toss the salad gently, and taste it. If desired, squeeze a bit of fresh lime over the top, and give it a couple of twists of freshly ground pepper.

Serves 6 as a side salad.

HEBREWS 13:1-2

Let mutual love continue. Do not neglect to show hospitality to strangers, for by doing that some have entertained angels without knowing it.

For further reading:
Genesis 18
Judges 6
Judges 13

REACH OUT   RESOLVE   REJOICE

REACH OUT	RESOLVE	REJOICE
How can you reach someone inside of your circles today?	How will you live out what God has shared with your heart in today's reading?	Count three blessings:
How can you reach outside of your circles today?		

Ways I fostered community today: Prayer Intentions

- ○ prayed for a friend
- ○ put down my phone in the presence of people
- ○ made plans to host a gathering
- ○ replied "yes" to an invitation
- ○ hugged someone important to me
- ○ shared a meal with someone special
- ○ wrote a letter by hand
- ○ set a table for more than myself
- ○ introduced myself to someone new
- ○ made time for these people:

- ○ other:

Asking God's help for myself:

Day Sixteen

D id you maybe just cringe a bit too? There's a conflict inside me when I read this passage. There's the part of me that squirms a bit at the idea of putting myself out there to a stranger, taking a risk and inviting someone I don't know into my cocoon of home. It's not safe and it's certainly not comfortable. It stretches me to think and then move beyond the pressing and sometimes overwhelming needs of the people I already know. *Lord, really? I can barely keep up with the needs of the kids I have, and you want me to go and add a few strangers in here too?*

Then there's the other part of me. This part of me reads an exhortation like this and thinks, *yes!* That is exactly what I want our home to be—a place where even strangers are welcome and made to feel loved and at home and where we can offer the fellowship and community that we ourselves long for. *Lord, you have given us so much. Who is it you want us to love and serve right now?*

You can guess which side makes me prouder. While there are most definitely seasons in life when God is calling us to more or less service outside of our immediate vocation, there is never a season when we aren't called to live out the works of mercy in some way. More often than not, living out that gospel message involves being pulled out of our comfort. It involves seeing every person around us as equally valuable to God and worthy of our time and resources. It involves becoming vulnerable to someone else, and even sometimes doing things that the world would say are foolish. This mindset of hospitality to strangers means placing our hearts, homes, and treasures at his service, and you know what? That very often involves risk. It did for the original hearers of this message too.

I don't think it's coincidence that just a few verses later, the Hebrews are encouraged not to be afraid of living out these exhortations. If the call didn't involve something a bit scary, there would be no need to tell them not to be afraid.

How are you called right now to welcome someone who might seem a bit risky? Is there a stranger in your life who needs you to welcome them in? Is there a way God is calling you to stretch outside your comfort level and take initiative to start a relationship?

Important to note here, the author of Hebrews is writing to, well, Hebrews. They are Jewish people well familiar with the Old Testament Scriptures, and they would have immediately understood the talk of entertaining angels as a direct reference to the story of Father Abraham and Sarah from Genesis 18. This was a story that many of them had probably heard told hundreds of times since youth, the story in which three "men" suddenly show up at the tent of Abraham and Sarah. Without hesitation they welcome these strangers in, treating them as the most honored of guests. These strangers from Genesis are understood to be two angels and the Lord himself visiting them. It is in the midst of being wined and dined by Abraham and Sarah that the strangers prophesy something Sarah finds so impossible that she laughs. She—old, disappointed, and seemingly cynical Sarah—will soon conceive and bear a son in her old age.

Understanding this context deepens our understanding of the later reference to entertaining angels in Hebrews. It's not that we're only supposed to offer hospitality to strangers because watch out! They might be angels in disguise! Angel or not, it is a Christian duty to offer hospitality to a visitor. But it serves as a reminder that when we do welcome in the stranger, we might be blessed beyond our wildest beliefs. In taking that risk and opening our lives and homes to the other, we might just see God himself break into our lives in a way we never thought possible. It's not clear from the text, but perhaps it was even because Abraham and Sarah welcomed those strangers that the Lord was then able to work such a miracle in their lives. Taking that risk, saying yes when he asks, and stepping forward even in the midst of fear and vulnerability open us up for him to work and speak powerfully in our lives. In ministering to them, that stranger might just become God's way of ministering to you.

Mary Haseltine

ROMANS 12:9-21

Let love be genuine; hate what is evil, hold fast to what is good; love one another with mutual affection; outdo one another in showing honor. Do not lag in zeal, be ardent in spirit, serve the Lord. Rejoice in hope, be patient in suffering, persevere in prayer. Contribute to the needs of the saints; extend hospitality to strangers. Bless those who persecute you; bless and do not curse them. Rejoice with those who rejoice, weep with those who weep. Live in harmony with one another; do not be haughty, but associate with the lowly; do not claim to be wiser than you are. Do not repay anyone evil for evil, but take thought for what is noble in the sight of all. If it is possible, so far as it depends on you, live peaceably with all. Beloved, never avenge yourselves, but leave room for the wrath of God; for it is written, "Vengeance is mine, I will repay, says the Lord." No, "if your enemies are hungry, feed them; if they are thirsty, give them something to drink; for by doing this you will heap burning coals on their heads." Do not be overcome by evil, but overcome evil with good.

For further reading:
2 Corinthians 8:1-15

REACH OUT   RESOLVE   REJOICE

How can you reach someone inside of your circles today?

How will you live out what God has shared with your heart in today's reading?

Count three blessings:

How can you reach outside of your circles today?

Ways I fostered community today: Prayer Intentions

- ○ prayed for a friend
- ○ put down my phone in the presence of people
- ○ made plans to host a gathering
- ○ replied "yes" to an invitation
- ○ hugged someone important to me
- ○ shared a meal with someone special
- ○ wrote a letter by hand
- ○ set a table for more than myself
- ○ introduced myself to someone new
- ○ made time for these people:

- ○ other:

Asking God's help for myself:

Day Seventeen

I set the folded piece of card stock on the nightstand and stood back to survey the scene. Pale blue walls, a soft new blanket, a blue and white patchwork quilt, meaningful art on the walls, and framed pictures of my adult children when they were younger—this was the room of my imagination. When my boys were little, I'd occasionally think of the far-off day when they'd come home with their wives and kids. Within the week, that day would be a reality. And the previous night, I'd initiated the final step of my preparations. I'd spent the night in our new guest room.

Long ago, I'd read that the best way to prepare for guests is to sleep in the room set aside for them so that any comfort issues would quickly become apparent. It's a brilliant strategy, really—one that is born of the truth that extending hospitality and building community are at the heart a matter of empathy. When you spend the night from a guest's perspective, you can think to provide a little table tent with the Wi-Fi password on the nightstand. You can remember to put a blanket on the end of the bed in case of the evening chill.

All the little touches are lovely. They are not hospitality though. Hospitality is the overflow of joy. Genuine hospitality happens when the hostess opens the doors to a place where the joy of Jesus has freed her to love other people. When joy overflows, it manifests itself in genuine charity. From where does the joy come?
From the cross.

When we want to live a Christian life of joy that overflows into an abundance of Christian love, we look "to Jesus the pioneer and perfecter of our faith, who for the sake of the joy that was set before him endured the cross, disregarding its shame, and has taken his seat at the right hand of the throne of God" (Hebrews 12:2). The woman who chooses to travel this road chooses to suffer with Christ. The road is a rocky one and she is guaranteed to cry on the journey. Along that road, she becomes aware of those who suffer. She learns to empathize. She recognizes need. And her joy in the ways the Lord meets her in her life compels her to meet others in their need, with love and mercy.

The table setting, the tasty treat, the decorative touches—those aren't what make us hospitable. Joy is. And it's joy in the life of Christ that propels us to use our time and our talents and our money and our energy to pump love into other people. Does that table tent matter? Yes! Is it good that it's beautifully lettered? Of course. But it matters because someone empathized. A person in love with Jesus stopped to consider what would bring her neighbor joy. She stopped to wonder in what tangible way she could share her own joy. Sometimes it looks like a table tent. Sometimes it's a covered dish and a bunch of flowers left on a doorstep. Sometimes it's just sitting quietly and saying nothing so that someone doesn't have to grieve alone. Hospitality is a soul in love who leans into the heart of another.

The hard road, the suffering, the grief known and the tears shed—they are all worth it because that share in the cross yields a woman whose arms are stretched out wide to envelop someone else in the love of Christ.

Elizabeth Foss

1 PETER 4:8-11

Above all, maintain constant love for one another, for love covers a multitude of sins. Be hospitable to one another without complaining. Like good stewards of the manifold grace of God, serve one another with whatever gift each of you has received. Whoever speaks must do so as one speaking the very words of God; whoever serves must do so with the strength that God supplies, so that God may be glorified in all things through Jesus Christ. To him belong the glory and the power forever and ever. Amen.

For further reading:
Luke 10:38-42
Galatians 3:3
Hebrews 11:6
Matthew 5:43-48

REACH OUT   RESOLVE   REJOICE

REACH OUT	RESOLVE	REJOICE
How can you reach someone inside of your circles today?	How will you live out what God has shared with your heart in today's reading?	Count three blessings:
How can you reach outside of your circles today?		

Ways I fostered community today: Prayer Intentions

- ○ prayed for a friend
- ○ put down my phone in the presence of people
- ○ made plans to host a gathering
- ○ replied "yes" to an invitation
- ○ hugged someone important to me
- ○ shared a meal with someone special
- ○ wrote a letter by hand
- ○ set a table for more than myself
- ○ introduced myself to someone new
- ○ made time for these people:

- ○ other:

Asking God's help for myself:

Day Eighteen

Not too long ago, a close friend unexpectedly showed up at my doorstep. We've always had an open-door policy—*mi casa es su casa*. But on this particular day, I was a hot mess and so was my house. I'd just awakened from a much-needed nap while my toddler was snoozing, and I was embarrassed my friend had caught me with sleep crust barnacled to my eyelids. Not to mention, my home—which on any given day, would probably pass a surprise inspection—was, at this moment, one step away from being declared a health hazard.

But this dear friend was not an inspector. She wasn't there to scrutinize my homemaking or napping skills. She was there to visit with me.

"Love covers a multitude of sins" (1 Peter 4:8). You know what else it covers? Toy flotsam. Mismatched shoes sprinkled across the floor. Dust bunnies. And a disheveled, imperfect hostess.

We live in an image-obsessed culture, and we often use everything from the décor of our homes to the meals we cook as benchmarks of our success.

We struggle to create perfect experiences for those we love instead of helping them to learn how to navigate the imperfect world we live in. We mistakenly fall into the trap of believing that a measure of our worth, and sometimes even our love for others, hinges upon how elaborate a party we can throw or whether or not we give our children or grandchildren the latest and greatest "things." Our culture's expectations for success and happiness are pushed so high that the simple beauty of an ordinary community gathering is lost and we feel ourselves or our homes are too inadequate to share with others.

We can't change the unrealistic expectations that social media, House Beautiful, and Pinterest place upon us, at least not overnight, but we can change what we value and how we view hospitality.

Caryll Houselander, a great spiritual writer, encourages us to embrace simplicity, saying,

> Stop striving to reach a goal that means becoming something the world admires, but which is not really worthwhile. Instead, we realize the things that really do contribute to our happiness, and work for those. For example, we cease to want to be rich, successful or popular, and want instead the things that satisfy our deeper instincts: to be at home, to make things with our hands, to have time to see and wonder at the beauty of the earth, to love and to be loved. (Caryll Houselander, *Wood of the Cradle, Wood of the Cross*)

How does this translate to your life? It means opening your heart and your home to others regardless of how you or your kitchen looks. It means worrying more about being hospitable and less about your culinary skills. It means giving priority to fellowship and peace. "Better is a dry morsel with quiet than a house full of feasting with strife" (Proverbs 17:1). Better a front door that yawns wide open to others despite the hand-me-down sofa inside.

My dear sisters in Christ, let us work to turn away from the pull of superficial, self-indulgent whims and redirect our focus toward God and the eternal. The world might not notice our little decisions to give and to love, especially if we're not striving to compete with Martha Stewart, Marie Kondo, or even that woman with the beautiful home and chic sartorial choices from our church.

Jesus is hungry for the humble over the fussy. He invites us to love simply and to give him—not Instagram—the glory. Sometimes Jesus is asking less from us; less of all that stuff that doesn't really matter means more of him and his love doled out to others on one imperfect paper plate at a time.

Kate Wicker

EPHESIANS 4:7-16

But each of us was given grace according to the measure of Christ's gift. Therefore it is said,

"When he ascended on high he made
captivity itself a captive;
he gave gifts to his people."

(When it says, "He ascended," what does it mean but that he had also descended into the lower parts of the earth? He who descended is the same one who ascended far above all the heavens, so that he might fill all things.) The gifts he gave were that some would be apostles, some prophets, some evangelists, some pastors and teachers, to equip the saints for the work of ministry, for building up the body of Christ, until all of us come to the unity of the faith and of the knowledge of the Son of God, to maturity, to the measure of the full stature of Christ. We must no longer be children, tossed to and fro and blown about by every wind of doctrine, by people's trickery, by their craftiness in deceitful scheming. But speaking the truth in love, we must grow up in every way into him who is the head, into Christ, from whom the whole body, joined and knit together by every ligament with which it is equipped, as each part is working properly, promotes the body's growth in building itself up in love.

For further reading:
1 Corinthians 4:1-7
1 Corinthians 12:13-31

Scripture Notes   Date:

REACH OUT   RESOLVE   REJOICE

How can you reach someone inside of your circles today?

How will you live out what God has shared with your heart in today's reading?

Count three blessings:

How can you reach outside of your circles today?

Ways I fostered community today: Prayer Intentions

○ prayed for a friend
○ put down my phone in the presence of people
○ made plans to host a gathering
○ replied "yes" to an invitation
○ hugged someone important to me
○ shared a meal with someone special
○ wrote a letter by hand
○ set a table for more than myself
○ introduced myself to someone new
○ made time for these people:

○ other:

Asking God's help for myself:

Day Nineteen

As my family grows, I'm increasingly given insight into how beautifully we are designed for life in community. My nine children stretch in age from ten to thirty years old. When we're all together for a holiday or a vacation, each of us falls into certain roles according to our gifts. Need to navigate a new place? Give the map to Nick and follow him. Want to bring beauty to the table before we sit down to a meal? Invite Kristin to collaborate with Katie and we're guaranteed a lovely tablescape. Need a diplomat to navigate an argument and smooth out hurt feelings? Lexi does that beautifully. Too many competing opinions and agendas, and we really need a plan that pulls it together? My husband is the family executive. What's so interesting to me is that not all of these people recognize themselves in the roles they're called to play. Often, it is those of us closest to each individual who see their gifts and urge them to share with our little community.

I wonder how often we unknowingly disqualify ourselves from using our gifts for the greater good? We know what we like to do, and we recognize our gifts in the things we're good at doing, but with self-discernment can also come self-limitation. We lack confidence or we hesitate to step into a challenge. In an atmosphere of trust and unconditional love, we aren't likely to be as afraid. We maintain that love covers a multitude of sins, to be sure, and it also more than compensates for the inevitable missteps along the way as gifts are developed.

In an environment that is kind and open, each member—from the youngest to the wisest, but still learning—is encouraged to grow into what God intended. And each gift serves the community in a unique and irreplaceable way. When a family or a faith community recognizes a gift and calls a member into the fullest service of that gift, something remarkable happens. Affirmation and encouragement on the part of one's friends nourish the gift.

The practice of coming alongside someone you love and helping them to see how God is calling is one that suits families well, but it's also a practice for other communities of faith. Beauty flourishes when we see how God desires to work within someone and when we help her recognize the gifts he graciously gives. The truest expression of this kind of community support comes when each member helps the other to prepare and practice their unique gifts. Parents do this with particular care, of course, as they educate their children. The practice is not limited to an older generation preparing a younger; my children teach me daily about my gifts and theirs. Encouragement of gifts expands to include friends who affirm and support, and it grows into an incredibly beautiful expression within a marriage.

When we choose vulnerability over self-protection, encouragement over disparagement, and love over fear, we mutually build a community made stronger by individual gifts. Constant love—the continuous laying down of one life for another—brings the strength of God to relationships. Stable, committed community offers to its members the room and the grace to grow into the truest expression of the gifts God gives. Nurturing communities don't just happen—whether in a marriage, a friendship, or a childhood. They are intentionally decided. In every moment over the lifetime of a relationship, we can choose to love and serve one another, mutually encouraging one another in the expression of gifts. Together we pray, we grow, and we learn the grace of God in the way we love one another.

As God has entered into a covenant with us, so do we honor one another. Every marriage, every family, and every community has its own unique story of the way it brings to life God's mercy and his glory in its midst. Every gathering of the faithful will offer to one another and to the world the individual gifts of each member that they've nurtured together.

Do you see the gifts in the people close to you? How can you help bring them to the world?

Elizabeth Foss

HEBREWS 10:19-25

Therefore, my friends, since we have confidence to enter the sanctuary by the blood of Jesus, by the new and living way that he opened for us through the curtain (that is, through his flesh), and since we have a great priest over the house of God, let us approach with a true heart in full assurance of faith, with our hearts sprinkled clean from an evil conscience and our bodies washed with pure water. Let us hold fast to the confession of our hope without wavering, for he who has promised is faithful. And let us consider how to provoke one another to love and good deeds, not neglecting to meet together, as is the habit of some, but encouraging one another, and all the more as you see the Day approaching.

For further reading:
Galatians 6:2
Psalm 133:1

REACH OUT   RESOLVE   REJOICE

How can you reach someone inside of your circles today?	**How will you live out what God has shared with your heart in today's reading?**	**Count three blessings:**
How can you reach outside of your circles today?		

Ways I fostered community today: Prayer Intentions

- ○ **prayed for a friend**
- ○ **put down my phone in the presence of people**
- ○ **made plans to host a gathering**
- ○ **replied "yes" to an invitation**
- ○ **hugged someone important to me**
- ○ **shared a meal with someone special**
- ○ **wrote a letter by hand**
- ○ **set a table for more than myself**
- ○ **introduced myself to someone new**
- ○ **made time for these people:**

- ○ **other:**

Asking God's help for myself:

Day Twenty

In the summer of 2004, a woman I had never met invited our family to stay in her home. It was a life-changing experience for me.

Back when my husband and I were the fiancé and I, we did the "responsible" thing and discussed how many kids we wanted to have. I'm from a two-kid family, his family has three. But we wanted a big family, so we decided upon the biggest number of kids I could imagine: four.

We also planned to wait to have any kids at all until Jim had finished graduate school and had a job. Well, it didn't quite work out that way. Just after grad school and three years after our wedding, we went back to Boston for his ten-year college reunion, and we brought two kids along with us.

My husband had been back in contact with his college mentor who still lived outside Boston; he and his wife invited us to stay with them for the weekend.

I'm sure Jim had mentioned the number of kids they have, but maybe I thought he was joking, or my brain just couldn't compute it, but I was surprised when it was . . . eleven. They have eleven kids. (Plus one they'd lost.)

Meeting them was an experience I'll never forget. These children, aged three to twenty-one, were helpful and polite and nice to each other and not . . . weird. I spent the whole weekend just in awe of everything. Especially things like their having only one TV, so they all sat in one room and flipped between a political talk show, a Red Sox game, and the Summer Olympics. All their teenagers (plus a couple of extras) were hanging out with the family on a weekend night, on purpose, and without grumbling.

Their life was so different from anything I'd ever seen. There was a chaos and a joyfulness and a rawness and a fullness to this home that I had never experienced in any of the homes of my friends growing up. And it's not like I caught them at some perfect moment in time either. This family was nothing if not real. Their second youngest, who has Down syndrome and celiac disease, had gotten into some "regular" cake, so her sisters were taking turns trying to help her through a bathroom visit; they forgot to pick someone up at baseball practice right up until a neighbor pulled into the driveway with him, and the dad looked wistfully at my son and told me that their first child had been about his age when he died in a household accident.

But their lives were linked together in a way that was both deep and effortless. I didn't know how they had what they had, but I knew I wanted it for my family.

I'm not even sure I connected all the dots at that point, that I understood that their joy came from authentic Catholic living and openness to life. I was in the midst of my "We're sure to figure out how this whole NFP thing works sooner or later" stage. I didn't know yet about the contentment that has come with being open to God's plan for my family, no matter if that was going to be the two kids I already had and that's it, or the nine that I've ended up with (so far).

We see this family only in yearly Christmas cards now. But I think of them often, and how this one act of hospitality, of meeting together in their home, forever changed my perspective on what family life could look like. Our own kids now range in age from one to sixteen. We genuinely enjoy each other's company for an evening, and we look for opportunities to welcome travelers into our home, to get a peek at how we live. And to see that we have only one TV.

Kendra Tierney

Selah is a Hebrew word found often in the psalms and a few times in Habakkuk. Scholars aren't absolutely certain what it means. It seems to be a musical or liturgical note—maybe a pause or crescendo.

We have set aside this space—this day—for you to use as your selah. Perhaps you pause here and just review what you have pondered thus far. Perhaps you rejoice here and use the space for shouts of praise. Or maybe you take the opportunity to fill in some gaps in the pages before this one.

It's your space.

Selah.

Give it meaning.

Check in.

TODAY'S DATE	PLACE OF PEACE:
___|___|___	_____

I'M FEELING

- ○ happy
- ○ excited
- ○ joyful

- ○ anxious
- ○ lonely
- ○ tired

- ○ connected
- ○ angry
- ○ sad

- ○ grateful
- ○ confused
- ○ peaceful

- ○ _____
- ○ _____
- ○ _____

In my community:	Working on my heart:
Missed connections + opportunities for togetherness:	Listening to:
	In my prayers:
Giving thanks for:	Hope for next week:

SIMPLE WAYS TO MAKE WELCOME

THAT ARE FREE, FUN, AND GOOD FOR YOUR SOUL

GREET THEM AT THE ENTRY

When hosting a gathering, it's easy to get caught up in the details of perfection. The kitchen is a mess but your guests have arrived early. Take a break (turn the broiler off if you need to) and greet them at the door. Introduce them to anyone they might not know in your home. Offer to hang up their coats or throw them over a chair, whatever your style is.

OFFER A BEVERAGE

This doesn't need to be fancy. Sometimes a glass of water is the perfect start to a wonderful gathering. This begins your hospitality, creating a comfortable environment. Many people feel less awkward and more comfortable in a new space with a beverage in their hands.

GIVE A QUICK HOME TOUR

A home tour doesn't need to be elaborate, and in most cases it's not necessary to show them the entire home. Give your guests a feel of the floor plan so that they feel comfortable in their surroundings. If nothing else, be sure to point out where the bathroom is.

OFFER A SEAT + YOUR TIME

Take control of your gathering, get cozy, and offer a seat. If you're cooking a meal, offer them a seat in or around the kitchen. If you're entertaining a large group, be thoughtful and introduce them to the person they are seated next to.

Give your guests something no one can buy from a store: your time and attention. A sure way to make someone feel welcome is to dedicate the time and energy to them. This includes eye contact and undivided attention. Silence your phone, listen to them intently, sit down next to them if you can, and remember to address them genuinely and ask, *How are you, really?*

Let Yourself Be Vulnerable

let your

light

shine

Let Yourself Be Vulnerable

SCRIPTURE MEMORY

"You are the light of the world. A city built on a hill cannot be hid. No one after lighting a lamp puts it under the bushel basket, but on the lampstand, and it gives light to all in the house. In the same way, let your light shine before others, so that they may see your good works and give glory to your Father in heaven."

MATTHEW 5:14-16

I will practice Scripture memory by
- ○ Praying
- ○ Writing
- ○ Speaking
- ○ Reading
- ○ Other: _____

FAIRLY HEALTHY COOKIES

Ingredients

- ○ ½ cup natural almond butter (no salt or sugar added)

- ○ ⅓ cup honey

- ○ 2 large eggs

- ○ ½ cup flaxseed meal

- ○ 1 cup rolled oats

- ○ ½ teaspoon ground cinnamon

- ○ ½ teaspoon salt

- ○ 1 teaspoon vanilla extract

- ○ ½ cup mini semisweet chocolate chips

- ○ ¼ cup chopped pecans

- ○ 1 cup finely ground oat flour (or substitute whole wheat flour)

- ○ ½ teaspoon baking powder

It's nice to keep the cookie jar full. Baking makes your house smell happy, and rare is the person who can resist the love in a cookie. These are made with one eye on nutrition and they're not overly sweet so that no one feels too terribly guilty if they eat them for breakfast.

Directions

Preheat the oven to 350°F and line a baking sheet with parchment paper.

In a stand mixer, beat the nut butter and honey until smooth. Add the vanilla and beat briefly.

Beat in the eggs until the mixture is fluffy.

Beat in the flaxseed meal and let the whole mixture sit while you combine the dry ingredients. It's good for the flax to sit in the wet ingredients for a few minutes.

Combine the oats, mini chocolate chips, cinnamon, salt, flour, and baking powder in a medium bowl.

Add the oat mixture to the nut butter mixture, gently stirring to combine.

Chill for half an hour.

Take a generous heaping tablespoon of dough, roll into a ball, and flatten slightly onto the baking sheet. Repeat with the rest of the dough, spacing the flattened balls about 1 inch apart. These cookies do not spread very much.

Bake until golden brown on the bottom, 6 to 8 minutes. Transfer the cookies to a wire rack to cool completely.

Makes about 18 cookies

ACTS 28:23-30

After they had set a day to meet with him, they came to him at his lodgings in great numbers. From morning until evening he explained the matter to them, testifying to the kingdom of God and trying to convince them about Jesus both from the law of Moses and from the prophets. Some were convinced by what he had said, while others refused to believe. So they disagreed with each other; and as they were leaving, Paul made one further statement: "The Holy Spirit was right in saying to your ancestors through the prophet Isaiah,

'Go to this people and say,
You will indeed listen, but never
    understand,
    and you will indeed look, but never
        perceive.
For this people's heart has grown dull,
    and their ears are hard of hearing,
        and they have shut their eyes;
        so that they might not look with
            their eyes,
    and listen with their ears,
and understand with their heart and
    turn—
    and I would heal them.'

Let it be known to you then that this salvation of God has been sent to the Gentiles; they will listen."
He lived there two whole years at his own expense and welcomed all who came to him.

For further reading:
2 Timothy 2:20-26

REACH OUT   RESOLVE   REJOICE

REACH OUT	RESOLVE	REJOICE
How can you reach someone inside of your circles today?	How will you live out what God has shared with your heart in today's reading?	Count three blessings:
How can you reach outside of your circles today?		

Ways I fostered community today: Prayer Intentions

- ○ prayed for a friend
- ○ put down my phone in the presence of people
- ○ made plans to host a gathering
- ○ replied "yes" to an invitation
- ○ hugged someone important to me
- ○ shared a meal with someone special
- ○ wrote a letter by hand
- ○ set a table for more than myself
- ○ introduced myself to someone new
- ○ made time for these people:

- ○ other:

Asking God's help for myself:

Day Twenty-Three

In today's readings, we find St. Paul preaching while under house arrest and not allowing his circumstances to impede him from spreading the gospel of life. His doors were always open, welcoming Jews and Gentiles alike, as he shared all that the Lord had done for him and was waiting to do for them.

As the Scripture reveals, it was not always easy, especially when those who came did not receive the word of the Lord with an open heart or open ears. I can imagine how his limitations must have frustrated St. Paul. His movements were so restricted, yet he had been called to evangelize. But St. Paul found a way to preach, through the writing of his letters to the outlying churches and by sharing with his visitors. He persisted in his mission to teach and love. He understood that God would bring all who needed to come to his door so he could teach the truth.

This scene speaks to my heart—the imperfection of it all, the boldness with which St. Paul shares his message even though he cannot leave those four walls. It takes me back to a season in my life when my daughter Courtney's health was so fragile that the only places I took her were medical appointments and Sunday Mass. The remainder of the time, we were home. For some, that might sound like a blessing, but for an extrovert like me, it was an extremely difficult season. What helped sustain me through the loneliness and isolation was my open-door policy. If you were well and you wanted to visit, my door was open, fresh muffins were made, and the coffee was hot. If I couldn't go out into the world because my daughter needed me home, then I would do my darndest to bring the world to me.

It was my way of spreading the gospel of life. We lived an isolated life, and many friends and neighbors had no idea what it was like to care for a severely disabled person. By opening the door and allowing the outside in, we made ourselves vulnerable to the world, exposing hearts that needed transformation and grace. In return, those who visited us opened themselves up, allowing us to love them right where they were. My life was transformed, one visitor at a time.

Those years were good, my friends. When you welcome people into your own sphere and from there serve one another, God will bless that abundantly. He will bring the right people to your doorstep whom you can encourage and who will encourage you to keep fighting the good fight and not lose faith. This is community in its purest form. My girlfriends and I prayed with and for each other. We discussed family issues and offered counsel to one another. In the confines of my home, we took the time to truly see the other without the many distractions of life.

There was usually laundry on the sofa, various dust bunnies floating about, and always dishes in the sink. Some days Courtney would have seizure after seizure and our guest would simply sit with me and be present in the distress. To know I was not alone in that moment made all the difference. None of these things stopped me from opening the door as wide as I could with a smile and open arms. I made what some might call my prison into a domestic church where the sick and tired could rest and be restored for the fight to come, myself included—just like I imagine St. Paul did.

Here's the thing about building community: it's never going to look like you want it to. There will be imperfect situations filled with awkwardness and times of frustration. But if we remain true to who God made us to be and trust that whomever he brings to our door was meant to be there, it's in those vulnerable moments when the truth of the gospel shines through. That's where community is born and mercy is shown as we become the face of Christ to one another.

Mary Lenaburg

JUDE 1:17-25

But you, beloved, must remember the predictions of the apostles of our Lord Jesus Christ; for they said to you, "In the last time there will be scoffers, indulging their own ungodly lusts." It is these worldly people, devoid of the Spirit, who are causing divisions. But you, beloved, build yourselves up on your most holy faith; pray in the Holy Spirit; keep yourselves in the love of God; look forward to the mercy of our Lord Jesus Christ that leads to eternal life. And have mercy on some who are wavering; save others by snatching them out of the fire; and have mercy on still others with fear, hating even the tunic defiled by their bodies.

Now to him who is able to keep you from falling, and to make you stand without blemish in the presence of his glory with rejoicing, to the only God our Savior, through Jesus Christ our Lord, be glory, majesty, power, and authority, before all time and now and forever. Amen.

For further reading:
Colossians 2:14
Romans 8:9

REACH OUT   RESOLVE   REJOICE

How can you reach someone inside of your circles today?

How will you live out what God has shared with your heart in today's reading?

Count three blessings:

How can you reach outside of your circles today?

Ways I fostered community today: Prayer Intentions

- ○ prayed for a friend
- ○ put down my phone in the presence of people
- ○ made plans to host a gathering
- ○ replied "yes" to an invitation
- ○ hugged someone important to me
- ○ shared a meal with someone special
- ○ wrote a letter by hand
- ○ set a table for more than myself
- ○ introduced myself to someone new
- ○ made time for these people:

- ○ other:

Asking God's help for myself:

Day Twenty-Four

My first day living in a L'Arche community home, where people with and without mental disabilities share life, I locked myself in the bathroom and cried. I had never felt so overwhelmed and uncomfortable in my life. It was chaotic merely being in a house shared by eight people, and totally daunting to be asked to jump in and help manage that house and assist the core members of the community—those with disabilities—with their daily lives.

Yet I tried my best to act like I knew exactly what I was doing. In my desire to appear useful, I offered help, never asking for it myself. In my desire to seem capable, I did things as I saw best, paying little attention to how they were already done. And in my desire to seem confident, I hid my fear, loneliness, and insecurity.

But I continued to feel overwhelmed, and it only got worse when one core member, Marie, began directing her frustration at me. She was grieving the loss of a beloved community member who'd left to get married, and since I had taken that member's place, I was the obvious target for Marie's emotions. She sighed loudly every time I entered the room, refused my offers of help, and usually ended up screaming at me before breakfast was over each day.

My time at L'Arche briefly overlapped with the community member who'd left, and I'd seen the natural way she interacted with everyone, particularly Marie. And so, unsure of what else to do, I decided to try my best to act like her. I pretended to be as bubbly and easygoing as she was, though I'm generally shy and serious. I acted goofy like her, even though I felt ridiculous the whole time. And one evening, I even tried to affectionately refer to Marie as "girlfriend," just as I'd heard the other community member do many times. But as soon as the nickname awkwardly left my mouth, I knew that I'd gone too far.

After a long pause, Marie screamed at me louder than ever, and I started to cry, exhausted from hiding how much her rejection hurt and how completely lost I felt. To my surprise, she also burst into tears and then softly said, "That's *her* name for me." As we stood there, I suddenly understood how that affectionate nickname had been born of an authentic relationship built on mutual vulnerability — which I hadn't been brave enough to offer Marie, or anyone else in the house, for that matter.

That tumultuous start to what ended up being a wonderful friendship and life-changing experience at L'Arche illustrates the wisdom of St. Jude's call for Christians to build themselves up on their most holy faith. The world tells us to measure our success by efficiency and quantity. But to maintain peace in our chaotic home, we had to focus on relationships, even if less got done and everything took a little longer. The world measures us by what things or positions we possess. But all that really mattered in our community was whether or not we would accept and love our fellow members and allow them to accept and love us in return. The world tells us to hide our weaknesses. But in L'Arche, we had to embrace them and reciprocate vulnerability with vulnerability in order to build meaningful relationships.

In sharing our brokenness, the other community members and I came to understand our great need for one another and for God. But away from countercultural communities like L'Arche, we must take care to avoid falling for the lie that we don't need each other, and that we don't need God. The world often feeds us a message of self-reliance, but God calls us to rely on one other, and on him. Supported by community, we are called to recognize our brokenness, repent when it leads us to sin, and continuously return to God, who awaits us with unending mercy.

For years, I've kept a replica of a candleholder that we had in my first L'Arche home on our dinner table. It's a circle formed by bodies holding hands, and whenever I see it, I'm reminded of our call to form community with those around us, and how doing so will always take a willingness to be vulnerable and authentic. It will mean facing rejection at times, and it will often feel awkward or uncomfortable at first. But those hard-won, soul-to-soul connections will strengthen our faith and allow us to experience life-giving acceptance and love.

Allison McGinley

1 CORINTHIANS 12:20-31

As it is, there are many members, yet one body. The eye cannot say to the hand, "I have no need of you," nor again the head to the feet, "I have no need of you." On the contrary, the members of the body that seem to be weaker are indispensable, and those members of the body that we think less honorable we clothe with greater honor, and our less respectable members are treated with greater respect; whereas our more respectable members do not need this. But God has so arranged the body, giving the greater honor to the inferior member, that there may be no dissension within the body, but the members may have the same care for one another. If one member suffers, all suffer together with it; if one member is honored, all rejoice together with it.

Now you are the body of Christ and individually members of it. And God has appointed in the church first apostles, second prophets, third teachers; then deeds of power, then gifts of healing, forms of assistance, forms of leadership, various kinds of tongues. Are all apostles? Are all prophets? Are all teachers? Do all work miracles? Do all possess gifts of healing? Do all speak in tongues? Do all interpret? But strive for the greater gifts. And I will show you a still more excellent way.

For further reading:
1 Corinthians 10:16-17

REACH OUT   RESOLVE   REJOICE

How can you reach someone inside of your circles today?

How will you live out what God has shared with your heart in today's reading?

Count three blessings:

How can you reach outside of your circles today?

Ways I fostered community today: Prayer Intentions

- ○ prayed for a friend
- ○ put down my phone in the presence of people
- ○ made plans to host a gathering
- ○ replied "yes" to an invitation
- ○ hugged someone important to me
- ○ shared a meal with someone special
- ○ wrote a letter by hand
- ○ set a table for more than myself
- ○ introduced myself to someone new
- ○ made time for these people:

- ○ other:

Asking God's help for myself:

Day Twenty-Five

For long years, I lived my life as "the hands and feet of Christ" in the mission field. I knew what my role in the body of Christ was, and I was comfortable with it. Since I returned to life in the United States nearly two years ago, things have looked much, much different. In less than two years, we have transitioned five kids back to life in the States and into attending traditional school for the first time in their lives. I have worked hard to recover from burnout and complex PTSD and to learn to manage my bipolar disorder, sometimes less successfully than others. I lost my mother, stepfather, and closest aunt in a two-month period. I was unemployed for six months. I have had planned and emergency surgeries. And our family has navigated a difficult and tumultuous divorce. It's been very, very hard.

Our move back to the States was based primarily on a job opportunity for me in Indiana, a place where we have no family but had a small core group of friends who were willing to welcome us. There are days I wonder if they would have been less willing had they known what these two years were going to bring. Over and over I have found myself in need of these friends. Over and over I have been, to my own thinking, an "inferior member" (1 Corinthians 12:24) of the body of Christ, needing coverage and support, reliant upon help rather than being the reliable help I had grown so accustomed to being for others.

I have wished my own neediness away more times than I can count. The transition from being hands and feet to being a broken leg, an ear with a cancerous lesion, a uterus with unhealthy growth, lungs infected with pneumonia, a heart hemorrhaging with grief—well, it has challenged me. And it has also changed me. Because what I have come to learn is that the body of Christ needs me. Period. It doesn't only need me when I am the strong one. It doesn't only need me when I can pull my own weight. It doesn't need me to always be a hand or a foot in its functioning.

The body of Christ is a living organism and, unlike a human body, its cellular makeup is mutable. A hand can, in an instant, become an eye that in turn can become a skin cell that in turn can become a lung, simply doing its best to remember to breathe. And when a hand that is in need of rest or recovery refuses to allow itself to step back into another role, the body loses some of its functionality. Because the parts of the body are meant to serve one another first, so that the body as a whole can then go serve the world in which it lives and moves and has its being.

In these last two years, a community of hands and feet and eyes and ears has come again and again to my rescue. They have stood outside of operating rooms. They have washed dishes and cooked meals and cared for kids. They have listened to me cry and reminded me to take my medication. They have sent money to pay the electric bill and waited anxiously with me for court orders. They have done the very hard work of covering me while I hurt and while I healed. Together, we have been the body of Christ. Had they refused to step into their roles, I would have suffered unbearably more. And had I refused to accept my own role, they would have been less for it.

We see so much division in the body of Christ in the world of social media. But there is another kind of dissension that can hurt the functioning of the body. That is the temptation to dissent in the role we are being asked to play in the moment, especially when we see that role as less desirable. What the last couple of years has taught me is that I am valuable to the body of Christ as I am, with what I have, where I find myself. And that I can trust that that body will rejoice in what I have to give when I am able to give, and run to cover me in its love when I am naked and vulnerable and in pain. Today I am the hands, tomorrow a lung struggling to breathe. Always needed. Always essential. This is the body of Christ. And it is beautiful.

Colleen Connell

LUKE 5:1-11

Once while Jesus was standing beside the lake of Gennesaret, and the crowd was pressing in on him to hear the word of God, he saw two boats there at the shore of the lake; the fishermen had gone out of them and were washing their nets. He got into one of the boats, the one belonging to Simon, and asked him to put out a little way from the shore. Then he sat down and taught the crowds from the boat. When he had finished speaking, he said to Simon, "Put out into the deep water and let down your nets for a catch." Simon answered, "Master, we have worked all night long but have caught nothing. Yet if you say so, I will let down the nets." When they had done this, they caught so many fish that their nets were beginning to break. So they signaled their partners in the other boat to come and help them. And they came and filled both boats, so that they began to sink. But when Simon Peter saw it, he fell down at Jesus' knees, saying, "Go away from me, Lord, for I am a sinful man!" For he and all who were with him were amazed at the catch of fish that they had taken; and so also were James and John, sons of Zebedee, who were partners with Simon. Then Jesus said to Simon, "Do not be afraid; from now on you will be catching people." When they had brought their boats to shore, they left everything and followed him.

For further reading:
Matthew 16:16-23
Matthew 14:28
Mark 1:20

REACH OUT   RESOLVE   REJOICE

How can you reach someone inside of your circles today?

How will you live out what God has shared with your heart in today's reading?

Count three blessings:

How can you reach outside of your circles today?

Ways I fostered community today: Prayer Intentions

- ○ prayed for a friend
- ○ put down my phone in the presence of people
- ○ made plans to host a gathering
- ○ replied "yes" to an invitation
- ○ hugged someone important to me
- ○ shared a meal with someone special
- ○ wrote a letter by hand
- ○ set a table for more than myself
- ○ introduced myself to someone new
- ○ made time for these people:

- ○ other:

Asking God's help for myself:

P eter had been out all night fishing and had come to shore exhausted and frustrated, his whole sleepless night having been a waste. When Jesus asked him to row him out a little way, Peter must have been annoyed, dozing as his Lord taught the crowds. And then Jesus, the land-loving carpenter, gave this generally successful fisherman a tip on how to fish. "Lower your nets," he said, right in the middle of the day when any amateur knew that fish wouldn't bite in the Sea of Galilee.

Peter voiced his doubts but put out his net. He was enough of a believer already to obey, though not yet faithful enough to trust. When his nets were filled, he must have been even more shocked than delighted—and given what such a catch would have been worth, that's saying a lot.

The Peter we see bumbling through the Gospels ought to have pulled every muscle in his body trying to pull in the catch himself. He was a tough guy, self-sufficient and successful, a man who would later rebuke Jesus mere moments after declaring him to be the Messiah (Matthew 16:16-23). Peter was the kind of guy who saw Jesus walking on water and had the audacity to try to join him (14:28). He was proud and impetuous, and it's in keeping with his character to attempt the impossible in order to save face.

But he didn't. Peter faced an overwhelming task and asked for help. He called to his partners, James and John, who came over to pull in the nets alongside him. When Jesus called Peter to follow him a few verses later, James and John accompanied him, leaving their boat (and their father) behind (Mark 1:20).

Which means that it's possible that the only reason we have the Gospel of St. John is because Peter was weak and asked for help.

Now, perhaps Jesus would have called John either way. But maybe not. Maybe 1 John and Revelation and the prologue of John's Gospel are fruits of Peter's momentary realization that he couldn't follow Jesus alone, that he needed help.

If Peter had powered through, insisting on his own sufficiency (or, perhaps, worried that he'd be a burden if he asked for help), the world might be dramatically the poorer for it.

It's very easy to convince ourselves that we shouldn't burden others, that their assistance would be too much to demand or that we don't really need it in the first place. It's easy to try to push through depressive episodes or to give up on family prayer rather than sit down with a friend and share our struggles. We think that holiness means self-sufficiency, that the saints must surely have been content to rely fully on God with no cousin or best friend or therapist as a mediator.

But that's not the testimony of Scripture, nor is it the witness of the saints. Peter needed help. Even Jesus begged his friends to stay awake and pray with him in the Garden of Gethsemane.

It often takes great humility to depend on the generosity of our friends. We feel needy, inadequate. We're convinced we are a burden. But what if our plea for help is exactly what they need to lead them to Jesus? What if in insisting on going it alone we deprive them of the encounter with Christ that might have transformed them forever?

Our God is powerful enough that he is able to allow our needs for the sake of others' salvation or sanctification or healing. If there's one thing I've learned in seven years of living out of my car, it's that God is able to supply other people's needs through their willingness to supply mine. Trust that when you're willing to ask for help, God is blessing your benefactor just as much as he's blessing you. Who might need you to be needy today?

Meg Hunter-Kilmer

MATTHEW 5:14-16

"You are the light of the world. A city built on a hill cannot be hid. No one after lighting a lamp puts it under the bushel basket, but on the lampstand, and it gives light to all in the house. In the same way, let your light shine before others, so that they may see your good works and give glory to your Father in heaven."

For further reading:
Romans 1:16-17

REACH OUT	RESOLVE	REJOICE
How can you reach someone inside of your circles today?	How will you live out what God has shared with your heart in today's reading?	Count three blessings:
How can you reach outside of your circles today?		

Ways I fostered community today: Prayer Intentions

○ prayed for a friend
○ put down my phone in the presence of people
○ made plans to host a gathering
○ replied "yes" to an invitation
○ hugged someone important to me
○ shared a meal with someone special
○ wrote a letter by hand
○ set a table for more than myself
○ introduced myself to someone new
○ made time for these people:

○ other:

Asking God's help for myself:

Day Twenty-Seven

Some people choose life verses. I have never been able to select just one scriptural passage as my favorite; I cannot narrow it to just one to envelop me day in and day out. Instead, I find myself claiming one, and then another, never letting go of the one before it. But I do have a "life quote"—a single passage from literature that so resonates that I revisit it every day and I hold it up as a standard.

> We do not draw people to Christ by loudly discrediting what they believe, by telling them how wrong they are and how right we are, but by showing them a light that is so lovely that they want with all their hearts to know the source of it. (Madeleine L'Engle, *Walking on Water*)

And so, perhaps I do have a life verse after all. Maybe it's the city on the hill verses. But I wrestle with the image. Because the city is on a hill, I picture it set apart, gated perhaps, just out of reach. Its light is there for the people below, but in my imagination, the city itself is not.

I have it all wrong, of course. The city on the hill that Jesus shared is a diverse community of people of all nations living together with a charism of hospitality that is oriented towards gathering more into its fold. We are light bearers, cheerfully swinging lanterns as we scramble down the hill to the people in the valley below.

The people of God will come forth from the city, right through those gates, and they will speak truth and grace, while pursuing justice and mercy. Not at all hunkered down up on the hill, the people of God will process on beams of light into a dark culture.

The citizens of the city will be known by their love. The light bearers are the wise teachers. They are the diligent workers, the excellent leaders, the compassionate healers. People from the city on the hill turn the other cheek and persevere under persecution. In continuous, humble service to the valley, the Christians are the people who extend Christ's love. Citizens from the hilltop gather those who dwell in the valley. Because the light is so lovely, the valley dwellers cannot look away.

God isn't promising that you will be set down on a hill in the midst of such a city. He is asking you to be that city. You, personally. A one-person city on a hill. The people in your home and your neighborhood will be better for you and your good works because the glory of your Father in heaven will shine through them.

To be Christ in the world and to gather souls together in order to live as Jesus did begins with living for him in an obvious way. The light of love that is the Lord's shines through us in such a manner that it is unmistakable to those who see it. We are joyful and generous with that light, illuminating the darkest corners and bringing warmth to the coldest loneliness.

In order to gather community to yourself, make your life the living expression of Christ's goodness. Look for opportunities to make even the smallest of life-giving gestures. The habit and the practice will open your soul to new opportunities for extending hospitality in the truest sense of the word. Your light will flicker and then it will flame. And that flaming light will not let itself be hidden.

Elizabeth Foss

LET GO + BE
VULNERABLE

Taking the time to reflect on our own vulnerability allows us to see how we open up to others. On the following page, imagine you have three vases of various sizes. Each vase represents a different level of vulnerability. What would you fill each with?

Write out what vulnerabilities you would put into the following vases.

The things that stay between you and God.

The things that you share with people inside of your circles.

Anything you feel comfortable sharing freely with a stranger.

Selah

Selah is a Hebrew word found often in the psalms and a few times in Habakkuk. Scholars aren't absolutely certain what it means. It seems to be a musical or liturgical note—maybe a pause or crescendo.

We have set aside this space—this day—for you to use as your selah. Perhaps you pause here and just review what you have pondered thus far. Perhaps you rejoice here and use the space for shouts of praise. Or maybe you take the opportunity to fill in some gaps in the pages before this one.

It's your space.

Selah.

Give it meaning.

The End.

God will send forth his steadfast love
and his faithfulness"

PSALM 57:3

END DATE	PLACE
_____	_____	_____	

I'M FEELING

- ○ happy
- ○ excited
- ○ joyful

- ○ anxious
- ○ upset
- ○ tired

- ○ annoyed
- ○ angry
- ○ sad

- ○ grateful
- ○ confused
- ○ calm

- ○ _____
- ○ _____
- ○ _____

Scripture to share:

_____

Three new things I
discovered about God:

1

2

3

_____

Giving thanks for:

When did I study best?

_____

Where did I study best?

_____

Praying for:

_____

What's next for my
Scripture study?

Rachel Balducci is a book author, newspaper columnist, television talk show cohost, and a university communications professor. Her favorite mission, however, is being a wife and a mom. Rachel and her husband, Paul, have five sons and one daughter, and lately life with boys involves lots of food and lots of basketball. Rachel writes about the intersection of faith and family, and she thinks often about how cleaning her bathroom will make her a saint.

Colleen Connell is a bringer-upper-of-boys and wannabe saint who packs a little Louisiana spice with her wherever she goes. She currently serves at-risk families in her job as a social worker in Fort Wayne, Indiana, and spends copious hours on football and soccer fields yelling more loudly than all the other moms. She finds joy in the word, the world, and the wild wonder of everyday life.

Katie Curtis grew up in Chicago but moved to the East Coast in high school, and now lives in Portsmouth, NH with her giant Scottish husband and six kids (including one-year-old twin boys). A Midwest girl at heart, she loves her neighbors, coffee, and conversations that get deep. When she isn't writing or cooking, she is driving her kids to sports or getting gummed on by babies. Her ideal day includes a writing session, a Rosary, a run, a dance party with her kids, and everyone home for a yummy dinner.

Micaela Darr is a California girl, born and raised, with brief stints in Mexico, Spain, and South Korea. She's extroverted by nature, but being a mom of seven kids has driven her to appreciate having quiet alone time, too. Her husband, Kevin, is the best in the world, especially because he's exceedingly patient in regards to her harebrained schemes (see: living in South Korea). Micaela is disorganized by nature, but is also bound and determined to improve herself in that area and has done so with a modicum of success. She loves to read, watch good TV, and chat your ear off.

Elizabeth Foss is a morning person who relishes her time alone with the word as much as she loves the inevitable interruption by the first child to wake. There is something so hopeful about every new day! A wife, mother, and grandmother, she's happy curled up with a good book or tinkering with a turn of phrase. She alternates between giving up coffee and perfecting cold brew. Elizabeth would rather be outdoors than inside, and she especially loves long walks in the Virginia countryside that sometimes break into a run.

Kristin Foss is a self-taught artist, plant person, minimalist wannabe, and ENFP (who appreciates intimate gatherings). She loves a good street taco second to a loaded poke bowl, but most nights she's at home sharing a homemade dinner with her family. She gravitates toward bright, vibrant colors and everything feminine and joyful. She believes home is a priceless place, and there are no rules to your heart's idea of aesthetic beauty.

Rebecca Frech is a big-mouthed girl who comes from a long line of opinionated women. She's a Texas girl who smokes a mean brisket and is always happy to show off her smoke rings. A self-proclaimed history nerd, she bought the house behind the town library in order to support her book-a-night reading habit. When she's not cooking, gabbing, or reading, she spends her free time raising eight children, remodeling her historic home, and sneaking off to the gym to lift all the things!

Mary Haseltine is a thirty-something wife, mom, doula, and author who writes about motherhood, birth, babies, miscarriage, doulaing, marriage, faith, and any other deep thoughts that strike her fancy. She's a passionate lover of Jesus, Scripture, the Church, JPII's Theology of the Body, and her husband and six boys. When not swimming in a sea of testosterone, she can be found working with doula clients, escaping from the house for a (quiet!) coffee and writing session, or enjoying a much-needed glass of wine with girlfriends. She lives in an old farmhouse in western New York with a flock of chickens and a whole lot of dreams.

Meg Hunter-Kilmer is a hobo missionary who lives out of her car and travels around the world giving talks and retreats; in her heart, though, she lives in a house surrounded by lilacs in a small town in the South and spends her afternoons on the front porch with a stack of Young Adult princess books and a plate full of pastries. That not being an option, she spends much of her time making small talk, listening to audiobooks, and hunting down unlocked churches where she can make a holy hour. She hates bananas with a burning passion and used to keep a guitar pick in her wallet just in case—despite the fact that she doesn't play guitar.

Mary Lenaburg relishes entertaining. Her door is always open and the coffee hot. When traveling to speak, she loves to explore the local candy shops looking for the perfect dark chocolate fudge (with nuts is best). Mary spends her free time reading the latest best-selling murder mystery and baking her famous chocolate chip cookies, ensuring that the kitchen cookie jar is always full. Mary and her husband have been happily married for thirty years, finding joy among the ashes, having lost their disabled daughter, Courtney, in 2014. They live in Northern Virginia with their grown son, Jonathan.

Allison McGinley recently moved to the Philly suburbs with her husband and two kids, and is living her dream with a church, library, and diner within walking distance. She returned to her faith during college, and nothing has been the same ever since, in the best way. Writing is the way she processes life and discovers the beauty all around her, and she's been known to write in her closet in the middle of the night when the right words were suddenly found. She's happiest when taking photos of beautiful things, worshipping God through song, drinking a cup of coffee, or standing by the ocean.

Kendra Tierney believes that anything worth doing is worth overdoing. To that end, she has nine kids (so far), literally wrote the book on liturgical living in the home, and, in her spare time, is renovating the family's hundred-year-old Los Angeles-area home. Her favorite parts are the Adam and Eve-themed laundry closet—after all, laundry is their fault—and the cathedral-ceilinged attic storage room that she's converted into a home chapel, complete with donated pews, as well as stenciled ceiling, floor, and walls. She hopes to be done before the baby moves out.

Kate Wicker is a wife, mom of five, author, speaker, and a recovering perfectionist. She loves reading, running, shoes, God, and encouraging women to embrace the messiness of life instead of trying to cover it up, making excuses for it, or feeling ashamed of their brokenness or their home's sticky counters. From her home in Athens, Georgia, Kate strives every single, imperfect day to strike a balance between keeping it real and keeping it joyful.

True Friend

Whether we are nineteen or forty-nine, friendship with other women can enrich our lives and it can make us weep. How do we find friends who are kind and true? By becoming those friends ourselves! This beautiful book invites you to explore what God has to say about lasting friendships.

Call Me Blessed

Every day of this four-week study provides Scripture to get you started and notes for further Bible reading. Step by step, day by day, biblical reading and inspiring essays introduce you to nineteen women of the Bible whose stories bring to life the dignity and vocation of women of God throughout the ages. Consider the stories of these biblical women in the light of the gospel, and see how their truths beckon you to also become a woman of God.

Consider the Lilies

Specifically designed to be an encouragement when times are tough, this six-week study provides Scripture to get you started and notes for further Bible reading. You will find a daily devotion, some thoughts to consider as you journal, and a prayer prompt to dovetail with your reading. Step by step, day by day, these words console and bring clarity to the hard days. Maybe this is a difficult season in your life—you're overwhelmed by the burdens weighing you down, the crosses the the Lord has asked you to carry. This study is for you. It is full of the consolations of the Holy Spirit. Here, you will find a guidebook to what God is saying, how he is encouraging you to lament, to pour out your grief and your fears and your anger. Or maybe you're in a sweet spot. Life is really rather good right now. This study is for you, too. It makes you a better friend to the woman next to you, to the growing child who aches, to the spouse who despairs. And it buries words in your heart so that they are there, waiting, when the rain begins to fall. Because it will fall.

An intimate encounter with the Rosary, this lovely volume integrates Bible study, journaling, and thoughtful daily action prompts. You will grow in your appreciation and understanding of the beautiful, traditional Rosary devotion, while deepening your love for Jesus in the Gospels.

Ponder for Kids

Created especially for children, this book contains Bible stories for every mystery of the Rosary. Full of interesting things to do, the journal is bursting with discussion questions, personal prayer prompts, puzzles, and coloring pages. There are also nature study pages to create a botanical rosary.

Stories of Grace

Here you will find thirty-one days of Jesus' stories carefully collected for you. Along the way, we've provided meditation essays, journaling prompts, space for your notes and drawings, beautiful calligraphy pages, and prayers to draw you deeper into the parables Jesus told. Do you have eyes to see and ears to hear our Lord's stories of grace?

Rooted in Hope

A newly revised bestseller, *Rooted in Hope* is a thirty-three-day Advent and Christmas study that extends from November 30 to January 1. In a look at Scriptures that tell the stories of prominent biblical figures, this study echoes and expands upon the popular Advent tradition of a Jesse tree. For each day, you'll find Scripture, a devotional essay, pages for guided *lectio divina*, and space to organize your days. Journaling pages and useful planning pages feature clear and elegant design, exquisite hand-drawn illustrations, and gorgeous calligraphy. A handy companion for Advent and Christmas seasons, this book will become a treasured keepsake for the woman who uses it.

Above All is a Lenten devotional journal that includes daily Scripture passages (set in context with enlightening historical notes to deepen your understanding), as well as devotional essays, room to journal, and space to organize your time. There is a simple prompt for the ancient prayer form of *lectio divina* each day, as well as a separate page for the fifth stage, *Actio*, where the reader is encouraged to examine her conscience and offer forgiveness to herself and to others. *Above All* is designed to help you reflect on all aspects of your life, particularly those that you may have pushed to the back burner. It's filled with tools to help you discover which areas need greater care and tending, and is meant to inspire and motivate you to become your absolute truest self, so that come Easter, you can flourish as God intended. The entire study—both words and images—is carefully crafted so that women can share it with the men in their lives, too.

Flourish

To the people of Rome, the cultural center of the world at the time, St. Paul wrote the most comprehensive expression of the gospel. For us, the Book of Romans is a study of sin and guilt, loss and rescue. It is the essential gospel. An in-depth look at the entire Book of Romans, this study provides inspiration and structure to dig deeply into St. Paul's guidebook for the early Church—and for us who are the Church today.

Hosanna

Hosanna is a Lenten devotional journal that is a deep and wide study of the Gospel of Matthew. Each weekday, readers will find a simple prompt for journaling tuned to the heart of the ancient prayer form of *lectio divina*. Weekends are reserved for rest and for hiding his word in the hearts of those who love him. *Hosanna* is designed to help you reflect on all aspects of your life in light of Jesus' call to live for the kingdom of heaven. It's at once gentle and challenging—a journey with one of Jesus' closest followers that will bring you into the presence of our Lord, from his birth to his resurrection.

Bibliography

She Reads Truth Bible. Nashville: Holman Bible Publishers, 2017.

The Didache Bible with Commentaries Based on the Catechism of the Catholic Church.
    San Francisco: Ignatius Press, 2015.

The Navarre Bible: New Testament Expanded Edition. New York: Scepter Press, 2008.

Hahn, Scott, general editor. *Catholic Bible Dictionary*. New York: Doubleday Religion, 2009.

Hahn, Scott, editor, and Curtis Mitch, compiler. *Ignatius Catholic Study Bible: New Testament*.
    San Francisco: Ignatius Press, 2010.

Houselander, Caryll. *Wood of the Cradle, Wood of the Cross: The Little Way of the Infant Jesus*.
    Sophia Institute Press, 1995.

Krugh, Karen Lynn. "Seeing Christ in All People." www.catholicculture.org. 2016. Accessed
    February 2, 2016, https://www.catholicculture.org/culture/library/view.cfm?recnum=528.

L'Engle, Madeleine. *Walking on Water: Reflections on Faith and Art*. New York: Convergent Books,
2016.

Lewis, C. S. *The Weight of Glory: And Other Addresses*. San Francisco: HarperOne, 2001.

the WORD
among us ®
The *Spirit* of Catholic Living

This book was published by The Word Among Us. Since 1981, The Word Among Us has been answering the call of the Second Vatican Council to help Catholic laypeople encounter Christ in the Scriptures.

The name of our company comes from the prologue to the Gospel of John and reflects the vision and purpose of all of our publications: to be an instrument of the Spirit, whose desire is to manifest Jesus' presence in and to the children of God. In this way, we hope to contribute to the Church's ongoing mission of proclaiming the gospel to the world so that all people would know the love and mercy of our Lord and grow more deeply in their faith as missionary disciples.

Our monthly devotional magazine, *The Word Among Us*, features meditations on the daily and Sunday Mass readings and currently reaches more than one million Catholics in North America and another half-million Catholics in one hundred countries around the world. Our book division, The Word Among Us Press, publishes numerous books, Bible studies, and pamphlets that help Catholics grow in their faith.

To learn more about who we are and what we publish, visit us at www.wau.org. There you will find a variety of Catholic resources that will help you grow in your faith.

Embrace His Word, Listen to God . . .

www.wau.org